Lernkrimi Englisch

# A Scottish Murder Mystery

Cécile Birt

**Weitere Informationen zu Compact Lernkrimis finden Sie am Ende des Buches und unter www.lernkrimi.de.**

© Compact Verlag GmbH
Baierbrunner Straße 27, 81379 München
Ausgabe 2016
5. Auflage

Alle Rechte vorbehalten. Nachdruck, auch auszugsweise,
nur mit ausdrücklicher Genehmigung des Verlages gestattet.

Redaktion: Helga Aichele
Fachkorrektur: Fiona Cain
Produktion: Ute Hausleiter
Titelillustration: Karl Knospe
Lernkrimi-Logo: Carsten Abelbeck
Gestaltung: EKH Werbeagentur GbR, textum GmbH
Umschlaggestaltung: EKH Werbeagentur GbR, Hartmut Baier

ISBN 978-3-8174-8379-2
381748379/5

www.compactverlag.de, www.lernkrimi.de, www.facebook.com/lernkrimi

# Vorwort

Liebe Leserin, lieber Leser,

sicher zum Lernerfolg – mit Spaß und Spannung! Die Compact Lernkrimis mit ihrer Kombination aus Lektüre und didaktischem Übungsanteil eignen sich hervorragend, um breite Sprachkompetenzen in der Fremdsprache zu erwerben. Der Lerner wird dabei durch die spannende Handlung, das angemessene Sprachniveau und den stetig ansteigenden Schwierigkeitsgrad der Übungen gefördert und motiviert.
Entwickelt nach neuesten Erkenntnissen der Fremdsprachendidaktik, sind Compact Lernkrimis das ideale Medium für einen Lernerfolg im Selbststudium. Durch die kleinen Texteinheiten und den hohen Übungsanteil sind sie aber auch als Unterrichtslektüre bestens geeignet.

**So lernen Sie mit Compact Lernkrimis:**
- **Mit Begeisterung lernen:** Die packende Krimihandlung motiviert Sie beim Lesen des englischen Originaltextes.
- **Wissen intensivieren und erweitern:** Durch die Kombination aus didaktisierter Lektüre und textbezogenen Übungen testen und trainieren Sie Ihre Sprachkenntnisse effektiv. Vokabelangaben auf jeder Seite unterstützen Sie beim Lesen.
- **Systematisch lernen:** Knüpfen Sie an Ihr individuelles Sprachniveau an und setzen Sie eigene Lernziele – linear im Schwierigkeitsgrad ansteigend oder mit punktuellen Schwerpunkten von Grundwortschatz bis Hörverstehen.
- **Unabhängig sein:** Lernen Sie ganz individuell – wo und wann Sie wollen.

Viel Spaß beim **spannend Englisch lernen**
wünscht Ihnen

Prof. Dr. Christiane Neveling
Didaktik der romanischen Sprachen, Universität Leipzig

# Inhalt

Chapter 1: An Englishman in Glengowan ............................... 5
Chapter 2: Dead Men Tell No Tales ......................................... 21
Chapter 3: A Little Knowledge Is a Dangerous Thing ............ 34
Chapter 4: Follow My Footsteps ............................................... 49
Chapter 5: Ask No Questions, Hear No Lies .......................... 64
Chapter 6: Every Dog Has Its Day ............................................ 79
Chapter 7: The Truth Will Out .................................................. 94
Chapter 8: Pride Comes Before a Fall ..................................... 110
Final Test ..................................................................................... 127
Answers ....................................................................................... 131
Glossary ....................................................................................... 142
List of Exercises ......................................................................... 154

# Zu diesem Buch

Inspector Hudson macht Urlaub in Schottland. Doch statt Ruhe und Erholung am Loch Ness genießen zu können, ermittelt er schon bald in einem sehr schottischen Mordfall. Wer hatte ein Motiv, den gutmütigen Dudelsackspieler Willy heimtückisch zu ermorden? Und warum wurde dabei auch der Dudelsack gestohlen?
Hier ist Hudsons Spürsinn gefragt, aber die örtliche Polizei arbeitet nicht gerade gerne mit ihm zusammen, sondern würde den Fall am liebsten schnell zu den Akten legen ...

Die Ereignisse und die handelnden Personen in diesem Buch sind frei erfunden. Etwaige Ähnlichkeiten mit tatsächlichen Ereignissen oder lebenden Personen wären rein zufällig und unbeabsichtigt.

# 1. An Englishman in Glengowan

"Watch out, Miss Paddington!"
Inspector Hudson's hands gestured frantically to the road ahead. The car in front came to a sudden halt.
"Better take the next turning," Hudson said, slightly annoyed.

| | |
|---|---|
| dashboard | Armaturenbrett |
| disgruntled | verärgert, verstimmt |
| majestic | majestätisch |
| to chime | läuten |

He threw a concerned glance at the clock on the dashboard and let out a disgruntled sigh.
"Don't worry, Inspector," Miss Paddington reassured him, "I'll make sure you don't miss your train."
She swiftly turned the steering wheel and the little car catapulted through the changing traffic lights and joined the end of yet another traffic jam.
Through the early-morning fog, Inspector Hudson could just about make out the majestic silhouette of King's Cross railway station in the distance. In the warm orange glow of the streetlights, a swarm of businessmen and women hurried in and out of the station entrance. The bells in the clock tower chimed eight o'clock. Six minutes until his train was due to depart. Inspector Hudson was feeling decidedly nervous. He wasn't used to being late for anything.
"Perhaps you should let me out here, Miss Paddington," he suggested as he reached for the suitcase on the seat behind him. "It'll be quicker to walk."

| to engulf | umringen, verschlingen |
|---|---|
| commuter | Pendler |

"Yes, Inspector, of course. So sorry about the rush this morning. I didn't think there would be so much traffic. Let me just pull over."

"Quite all right, Miss Paddington," the inspector mumbled, trying to hide his slight annoyance. "Enjoy having the house to yourself."

He shut the car door and turned to cross the road.

"You'll be missed, Inspector."

Miss Paddington scrolled down the window and shouted out over the noise of the oncoming traffic. "Have a wonderful holiday and don't forget to call when…"

But the inspector had already been **engulfed** by a crowd of **commuters** and could no longer hear her.

**Exercise 1: Unscramble.** Bringen Sie die Buchstaben in die richtige Reihenfolge!

1. uerdsegt  _____

2. ronsipect  _____

3. odewrlufn  _____

4. usrenvo  _____

5. remtumoc  _____

6. styfliw  _____

7. camsitej  _____

"…Now departing from platform 1 is the 8:06 train to Inverness…," the loudspeakers **bellowed** as Inspector Hudson rushed towards the waiting train.

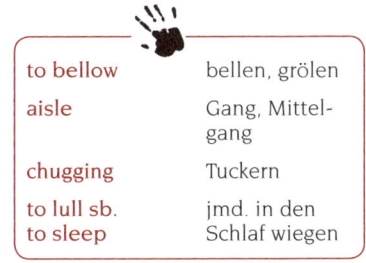

| | |
|---|---|
| to bellow | bellen, grölen |
| aisle | Gang, Mittelgang |
| chugging | Tuckern |
| to lull sb. to sleep | jmd. in den Schlaf wiegen |

He made his way towards platform 9 as quickly as he could, dodging through the crowds of commuters.

Just as the station master blew the final whistle, Hudson pulled out his ticket and stepped into the carriage.

"All aboard for Inverness!"

The doors slammed shut behind him, and the inspector squeezed along the **aisle** of the crowded train into a small compartment by the window.

A kindly-looking old lady was already sitting in one of the two seats. She looked up from her knitting and gave the inspector a friendly nod.

"Good morning," she smiled. "Travelling to Scotland? I'm going to visit my grandchildren. Little Jimmy is…"

"How nice," Inspector Hudson mumbled.

He pretended to listen but it had been a hectic morning, and he had been looking forward to enjoying the eight-hour train journey to Inverness with nothing but a cup of tea and a good book for company.

The old lady continued to chat away while he lifted his suitcase up onto the shelf above his seat and sat down opposite her. The train began to pull out of King's Cross station, and Inspector Hudson watched as the large Victorian houses sped past. Soon, the red-brick scenery gave way to the wide, open fields of the English countryside. The inspector leant his head against the window. The faint **chugging** of the engine and the soft clicking of the old lady's knitting needles gently **lulled him to sleep**.

**Exercise 2: Word order.** Bringen Sie die Wörter in die richtige Reihenfolge!

1. platform   train   from   8:06   to   departing   the   1   is   now   Inverness

   _____

2. to   my   going   I'm   grandchildren   visit

   _____

3. a   morning   hectic   had   it   been

   _____

4. away   lady   chat   old   the   to   continued

   _____

After what seemed like only a short nap, the inspector felt a bony hand on his shoulder shaking him awake.
"Wake up, sir!" the old lady whispered. "We're here. Welcome to Inverness!"
Inspector Hudson **squinted** in the dim light of the carriage. He glanced at his watch and then at the old lady standing before him. 4:15 p.m. The yellow scarf, which she had begun knitting at the start of their journey, was **trailing** along the floor behind her. He really had slept all the way. Hudson suppressed a chuckle. Sir Reginald must have been right: he clearly was in need of a good rest.

| to squint | blinzeln, die Augen zusammenkneifen |
| --- | --- |
| to trail | schleifen |

He thanked the little old lady and wished her a pleasant stay with her grandchildren before stepping off the train. A strong wind blew in from across the platform and the inspector was grateful for the extra coat Miss Paddington had insisted he pack.

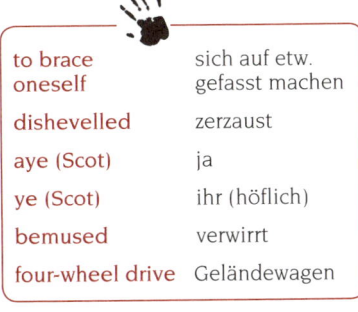

| | |
|---|---|
| to brace oneself | sich auf etw. gefasst machen |
| dishevelled | zerzaust |
| aye (Scot) | ja |
| ye (Scot) | ihr (höflich) |
| bemused | verwirrt |
| four-wheel drive | Geländewagen |

He buttoned up the collar and **braced himself** for the biting cold that was about to greet him at the station entrance. The inspector stepped out into the wintry sunset and headed for the taxi stand. A few snowflakes were beginning to fall but there were no taxis in sight.

A moment later, however, a dark, bearded figure came running towards him.

"Excuse me," the inspector shouted, waving his hand to catch the man's attention. "You don't happen to know what one has to do to get a taxi around here, do you?"

A weather-beaten face peered out from behind the **dishevelled** brown beard.

"**Aye**, an Englishman!" he exclaimed in a strong Scottish accent. "**Ye** must be Mr Hudson."

"Well, yes…," the inspector answered, a little **bemused** as to how this stranger knew his name.

"Jolly good," the bearded man continued, taking the inspector's suitcase from his hand. "Abraham Darling's my name. Dorothy asked me to pick you up and drive you down to Glengowan. Ye won't find any taxis around here today."

The man marched off towards a muddy green **four-wheel drive**.

"Thank you, Abraham, that's very thoughtful of Mrs Murdoch," the inspector replied, still somewhat confused. "Where are all the taxis then?"

He followed the rugged-looking man to the car and climbed into the passenger seat.

> **Exercise 3: Questions about the text.** Beantworten Sie die Fragen zum Text!
>
> 1. Apart from looking at his watch, how did Hudson know that he had been asleep for a long time?
>
> _____
>
> 2. Why has Hudson chosen to holiday in the Scottish Highlands?
>
> _____
>
> 3. Why was Hudson grateful for the extra coat that Miss Paddington had insisted on?
>
> _____
>
> 4. Did Inspector Hudson expect to be picked up?
>
> _____

| | |
|---|---|
| rugged | rau, markant |
| Burns Night | Geburtstag des schottischen Dichters Robert Burns |

"You chose a fine day to visit, Mr Hudson. The twenty-fifth of January is Burns Night! The villagers are all busy celebrating and the taxis are in high demand."

Abraham started the ignition and the car sped off through the muddy Inverness roads.

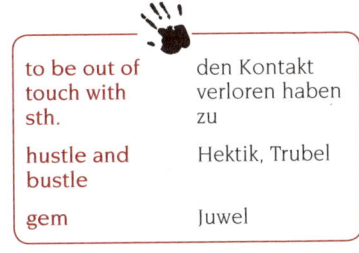

| | |
|---|---|
| to be out of touch with sth. | den Kontakt verloren haben zu |
| hustle and bustle | Hektik, Trubel |
| gem | Juwel |

"Burns Night, of course," Hudson muttered to himself. "I remember reading something about it in the papers this morning: a traditional celebration of the life of Scottish national poet Robert Burns."

"Right you are, Mr Hudson," Abraham was pleased that the English weren't entirely **out of touch with** Scottish tradition. "Just visiting, then?"

"Yes, just visiting," Hudson answered as he looked out over the snowy valleys. "I fancied a break as far away from the **hustle and bustle** of London as possible."

"And ye decided on Glengowan? A good choice, sir. It's a real **gem** of a village; one of the few that hasn't bought into the Loch Ness tourist trap. Nice and quiet, just how the locals like it."

"Sounds perfect," the inspector said with a smile.

"Though I'm afraid ye won't get much peace and quiet this evening. Glengowan is renowned for its lively Burns Night celebrations."

"Oh, I don't think I'll be joining in."

"Not joining in?" Abraham cried out in surprise. "I'm sure Mrs Murdoch won't hear of it."

"I was afraid you'd say that," replied the inspector, as his hopes of a quiet dinner and fine Scottish whisky by the fireplace faded. "So what exactly happens during these Burns Night celebrations?"

"Aye, I'll let ye find that out for yourself, Mr Hudson!" Abraham chuckled and turned down a bumpy lane towards a little village. "Here we are. Welcome to Glengowan! The most beautiful village in Scotland."

**Exercise 4: Translation.** Übersetzen Sie folgende Begriffe!

1. ignition　　＿＿＿＿＿＿＿＿＿＿＿＿

2. he muttered　＿＿＿＿＿＿＿＿＿＿＿＿

3. tourist trap　＿＿＿＿＿＿＿＿＿＿＿＿

4. peace and quiet　＿＿＿＿＿＿＿＿＿＿＿＿

Hudson wiped the condensation from the car window so that he could get a better view as they drove towards the hotel. The village was as picturesque as a Christmas postcard. The roofs of the **stone-clad** houses were topped with snow, and thick, white smoke **puffed** steadily from their chimneys. The narrow streets were lined with old-fashioned lanterns, and in the centre was an old church with an overgrown graveyard. He couldn't have dreamt of a more beautiful setting for his holiday.

Abraham took a sharp left into a gravel driveway, **jolting** the inspector out of his daydreams. Straight ahead was a large grey mansion house with a **carved** wooden sign swinging above the green door.

"The Loch Inn," Abraham announced. "Welcome!"

Hudson shuffled out of the car and **grimaced** as his newly-polished leather shoes were **submerged** by a deep puddle.

| | |
|---|---|
| stone-clad | mit Stein verkleidet |
| to puff | *hier:* aufsteigen; hinausblasen |
| to jolt sb. out of sth. | jmd. aus etw. aufrütteln |
| carved | geschnitzt |
| to grimace | das Gesicht verziehen |
| submerged | unter Wasser gesetzt |

"You'd better trade them in for a pair of **wellies**!" Abraham called out in a friendly tone. "Come in before you catch a chill."

| ⚡ wellies | Gummistiefel |
| log fire | Kaminfeuer |
| to scuffle | schlurfen |
| tartan | karierter Schottenstoff |
| jolly | fröhlich |

Hudson shook the water from his shoes and stepped into the warm entrance hall. It smelt of **log fires** and dried lavender and he felt immediately at ease in the Inn's homely surroundings.

"So, where's the lady of the house?" he asked, looking around.

"Just coming!"

The shrill voice of Dorothy Murdoch preceded the petite figure that **scuffled** out from behind the reception desk. She was dressed from top to toe in purple **tartan**, with a little purple ribbon in her grey curls.

**Exercise 5: Verb forms.** Lesen Sie weiter und unterstreichen Sie die richtige Variante!

"A pleasure to finally 1. met / meet you, Mr Hudson. I've so much been looking forward to 2. having / have you here. I'm sure it's not as fancy as what you're used to, but we'll do our best to make you 3. feeling / feel at home."

"I'm sure it'll be quite delightful, Mrs Murdoch."

The inspector 4. following / followed the **jolly** little landlady up a crooked flight of stairs and along the creaky corridor.

| | |
|---|---|
| four-poster bed | Himmelbett |
| Burns Supper | in Schottland ein jährliches Fest zu Ehren des Dichters Robert Burns |
| in dismay | entsetzt |
| array | große Anzahl |

"It's the third door on the left; our very best room. And please, call me Dorothy, everybody does."

She opened the door to a cosy room with a large **four-poster bed** in the centre and a window overlooking Loch Ness.

"Charming, Dorothy. I'm sure I'll never want to leave."

Hudson put his suitcase down by the roaring fire and proceeded to take off his wet shoes.

"What time shall I come down for dinner?" he asked.

"I'm afraid there'll be no dinner served at the hotel this evening, Mr Hudson. I'm sure Abraham must have mentioned that it's Burns Night tonight. All the villagers are gathering in the village hall for the **Burns Supper**. You will be joining us, won't you?"

"Actually, Dorothy, I'm afraid it's been a long day and I'm not really in the mood for…," the inspector began to make his excuses but was swiftly interrupted.

"Now, now, Mr Hudson. We can't have you here all by yourself while we're off having fun. Supper begins at 7 p.m. sharp in the village hall."

And with that, Dorothy closed the door behind her, leaving Hudson no time to disagree. It was already half past six, and after having a quick wash and slipping into his suit, the inspector headed back down the stairs. He stared **in dismay** at the large **array** of muddy Wellingtons in the hallway and pulled on the cleanest-looking pair he could find. A suit with wellies, that must be a first, the inspector thought to himself.

The Loch Inn was deathly quiet as the other hotel guests were already at the supper. Hudson buttoned up his coat, stepped into the dark, cold night and followed the footprints in the snow towards the village square.

**Exercise 6: Correct the mistakes.** Lesen Sie weiter und korrigieren Sie die sieben Fehler im folgenden Absatz!

As he approaches, the clinking of glasses and babble of happier voices grew louder. He could already see the villagers sitting at their candle-lit tables threw the large windows of the village hall.

There must be at little 200 people here, he thought as he entered the hall, and by the seems of it, I'm one of the only men not wearing a kilt. Hudson suddenly felt very out of space and was about to turn around to leave when Dorothy's familiar voice called out from a table to his right.

"Over here, Mr Hudson! We've saved a seat for you! Don't be shy, everyone's looked forward to meeting our new guest."

1. _____  2. _____
3. _____  4. _____
5. _____  6. _____
7. _____

Dorothy patted the seat next to hers and the inspector reluctantly obliged.

"Meet Father Angus and Duncan MacDougal," Dorothy introduced Hudson to two companionable-looking men. "Duncan runs the

| | |
|---|---|
| clinking | Klirren |
| babble | Geplapper, Murmeln |
| kilt | Schottenrock |
| reluctantly | ungern, widerstrebend |
| to oblige sb. | jmd. entgegenkommen |

| | |
|---|---|
| wool mill | Wollspinnerei |
| parish | Pfarrbezirk |
| abundance | Fülle, Vielzahl |
| in unison | gemeinsam |
| tumbler | Trinkglas |
| proceedings *pl* | Ablauf |

Glengowan **wool mill** and Father Angus is our much-loved **parish** priest."

"A pleasure to meet you, gentlemen."

The inspector was about to sit down when there was a huge round of applause and a tall, well-dressed man in his mid-forties climbed onto the stage in the centre of the room. A large, gold medallion was tied around his neck with a red ribbon and he held a glass of whisky in his hand.

"If I may have your attention, ladies and gentlemen."

The tall man cleared his throat before continuing. "For those of you visiting from neighbouring villages, or perhaps even further afield[i], my name is Quentin Cartwright. I'm the mayor of Glengowan, and I'd like to welcome you to our beautiful little village here on the shore of Loch Ness. As ever, we have some traditional Burns Night celebrations in store for you with song, dance and an **abundance** of food."

The congregation let out a heartfelt cheer and raised their glasses of whisky **in unison**. The mayor's speech continued for some time, and Hudson's mind began to wander as he observed the happy villagers.

> Das Idiom **far/further afield** bedeutet „weit/weiter entfernt".
> Dabei bezieht sich **afield** (wörtl.: im Felde) meist auf die Entfernung von zu Hause oder einen Aufbruch ins Unbekannte.

Every so often, Dorothy would give him a gentle nudge and they'd all stand to drink a sip of whisky from their **tumblers**. The inspector couldn't complain about that part of the **proceedings** and, after cheering a few toasts, he began to enter into the spirit of the Burns Night festivities.

**Exercise 7: Adjectives.** Lesen Sie weiter und unterstreichen Sie alle Adjektive!

After a traditional **grace** said by the mayor's wife, an almighty blast of Scottish music filled the hall. A **stocky** man with a **shock** of bright-red hair marched between the rows of tables playing his **bagpipes**.
"Fantastic!" exclaimed Hudson. "**The real McCoy**!"
"That's Willy," Dorothy shouted into his ear above the sound of the nearing bagpipes, "he's piping in the **haggis**."

"Piping in the haggis?" the inspector asked with a quizzical look.
"Aye, see those men behind Willy carrying a silver **platter**? That's the haggis, **neeps and tatties** we'll be eating for our dinner."

"Neeps and tatties?" Hudson was beginning to feel a little ignorant at his lack of local knowledge.
Dorothy only laughed. "**Turnips** and potatoes, Inspector. You'll see."
A large and rather unappetizing plate of unfamiliar food was laid before the inspector. All the guests took another sip of whisky and began to eat.
"Aren't you hungry, sir?" asked Father Angus from across the table.

| | |
|---|---|
| grace | *hier*: Tischgebet |
| stocky | untersetzt |
| shock (of hair) | Haarschopf |
| bagpipes *pl* | Dudelsack |
| ↯ the real McCoy | der wahre Jakob, das einzig Wahre |
| haggis (Scot) | schottisches Gericht aus Schafsinnereien |
| platter | Servierteller |
| neeps and tatties *pl* (Scot) | Rüben und Kartoffeln, typische Beilage zu Haggis |
| turnip | Weisrübe |

| | |
|---|---|
| innards *pl* | Innereien |
| rendition | Interpretation, Version |
| Auld Lang Syne (Scot) | wörtl. "die gute alte Zeit", ein bekanntes schottisches Lied, verfasst von Burns |
| to disperse | sich auflösen |
| tipsily | beschwipst |
| rectory | Pfarrhaus |
| verge | *hier*: Grünstreifen; Rand |

"Erm... Is haggis really made from sheep's **innards**?" Hudson's question came out a little more feebly than he would have liked.

"Indeed! From sheep's liver and lungs and all things nice, cooked up in a sheep's stomach. Now eat up before it gets cold!"

Hudson didn't want to offend the locals on his first day in the village, so he shut his eyes and took a bite of the haggis. To his astonishment, it tasted rather good, like well-seasoned sausage.

After the dinner, more speeches, and a jolly **rendition** of **Auld Lang Syne**, the guests began to **disperse** into the dark, snowy night. Inspector Hudson was deep in conversation with Mavis, who ran the village post office, when Father Angus got up to leave.

"Goodbye, Inspector. I hope you enjoy your stay!"

With a friendly wave, Father Angus made his way **tipsily** towards the **rectory**.

The streets were bustling with villagers on their way home from the party, and Father Angus could hear the odd car stuttering against the cold. What he didn't notice, however, was that as he pulled his coat tightly around him, his keys slipped out of his pocket and onto a small **verge** of grass. It wasn't until he reached the door of the rectory that he realized what must have happened and turned to retrace his steps. After a few moments, the moon emerged from behind a cloud and he thought he saw something glimmering on the roadside.

**Exercise 8: Hidden words.** In diesem Gitternetz sind sieben schottische Begriffe versteckt. Welche sind es?

| L | T | A | R | T | A | N | L |
|---|---|---|---|---|---|---|---|
| H | E | N | A | A | O | E | O |
| A | Z | D | U | T | E | E | C |
| G | U | K | H | T | I | P | H |
| G | X | I | Q | I | N | S | N |
| I | L | L | F | E | E | W | E |
| S | O | T | K | S | H | A | S |
| B | A | G | P | I | P | E | S |

1. _____  2. _____

3. _____  4. _____

5. _____  6. _____

7. _____

Father Angus reached out into the darkness to pick up his keys, but as he felt around for them, his hands grabbed hold of something warm and wet. As he took a step back to get a better look, he noticed that his hands were covered in blood.

Squinting through the moonlight, he saw a body lying face-down on the pavement. Father Angus knelt down and checked for a pulse but it was too late. He couldn't see the figure's face in the darkness but from the long tangle of hair, he knew instantly who it was.

# 2. Dead Men Tell No Tales

A few whiskies later, Hudson had also decided **to call it a night,** and he and Dorothy Murdoch were walking through the faintly-lit village

| | |
|---|---|
| to call it a night | Schluss machen |
| breadth | Umfang |
| intriguing | faszinierend |
| splendid | großartig |
| cassock | Soutane |

square towards the little lane that led to the Loch Inn.

"I see you got trapped by old Mavis, Mr Hudson. I hope she didn't keep you chatting too long. Mavis is certainly one for a bit of gossip, but she's a kind soul at heart."

"Not at all," Hudson replied. "We were having a very pleasant conversation. Her **breadth** of local knowledge is, as you say yourself, rather… impressive. I doubt there was a single one out of the two hundred guests about whom she didn't know a few **intriguing** personal facts."

"That's Mavis for you," Dorothy chuckled. "Well, I'm certainly glad you decided to join us for the Burns Supper. It was one of the finest Glengowan has seen in years. Don't you think Mayor Cartwright gave a **splendid** speech?"

"Yes, well, errr…"

Hudson was saved from having to answer Dorothy's question by the sound of Father Angus' voice echoing across the square.

"Help! Help!"

Dressed in his black **cassock**, it would have been almost impossible to make out Father Angus' figure in the darkness had it not

| ⚡ dog collar | Priesterkragen |
| battered | zusammenge-schlagen |
| gruff | rau |
| distressed | erschüttert |

been for his sparkling-white dog collar.

"Over here, Father!" Dorothy cried back. "What's wrong?"

"Oh thank goodness I've found you, Mrs Murdoch," Father Angus panted as he drew closer. "I'm afraid something terrible has happened…"

---

**Exercise 9: Odd one out.** Welches Wort ist das „schwarze Schaf"? Unterstreichen Sie!

1. afterwards   later   eventually   subsequently
2. breath   breadth   breathe   bread
3. intriguing   interesting   attractive   unfamiliar
4. illustrated   painted   draw   sketched

---

A short while later, Hudson was standing in the all-too-familiar blue flashing lights of police cars. Beside him lay the battered body of Willy, the red-headed bagpiper whose music he had enjoyed just a few hours previously.

"There's nothing to be seen here," the gruff Scottish voice of the police sergeant barked out to the crowd of villagers starting to gather around the body. "Best be on your way home now."

Familiar with such situations, it had been the inspector who had telephoned for the police and calmed down the distressed Dorothy. Driven by his police instinct, he had immediately taken a close look at Willy's lifeless body and the potential crime scene. But Hudson was also keen to remind himself that he was here on holiday and not on business.

The police sergeant walked a few steps towards the inspector, who was still comforting Dorothy.

| flustered | aufgeregt |
| to reciprocate | erwidern |

"Come on, Mum," he said, far more kindly. "You should be getting home as well. It's late and there's nothing we can do for Willy now."
"Mum?"
"Oh, yes, sorry, Mr Hudson," Dorothy said, a little flustered. "This is my son, Fergus."
"Sergeant Fergus Murdoch. A pleasure to meet you."
"Likewise," the inspector reciprocated. "I'm James Hudson. I'll see that Mrs Murdoch gets home safely."
And with that, the two of them walked towards the Loch Inn.

### Exercise 10: Verb forms. Lesen Sie weiter und ergänzen Sie die fehlenden Verbformen!

be   make   sleep   sit   rise   creep

The next morning, Hudson 1. _____ early after a sleepless night. Still in his pyjamas, he 2. _____ quietly down the creaky staircase and into the communal kitchen to 3. _____ himself a cup of tea.
"Trouble 4. _____, Mr Hudson?"
Startled, the inspector turned around. Sergeant Murdoch 5. _____ on the chair nearest the fireplace. There 6. _____ large, dark circles under his eyes.

| | |
|---|---|
| forensics | Gerichtsmedizin |
| morgue | Leichenhalle |
| ⚡ cuppa | Tasse Tee |
| ⚡ missus | Ehefrau |
| to linger | lungern |
| hit-and-run | Unfall mit Fahrerflucht |
| bewilderment | Verwirrung |

"Good morning, Sergeant," Hudson replied. "Yes, perhaps it was a little bit too much excitement for me last night. Either that or the whisky."

"I understand. I suppose it's not every day you come across a dead body," Sergeant Murdoch said with a yawn.

"No, not every day," Hudson said in half-truth, unsure as to whether or not he should reveal his profession to the policeman. "I have to say, it's a first for me as well. It took ages for **forensics** to get there, and it was 4 a.m. before we could take the body to the **morgue**. I've only just got in. Thought I'd have a **cuppa** before heading off to bed. Things aren't going so well between me and the **missus** and Mum doesn't mind me staying over every now and then when she's got a room spare."

"I'm sorry to hear it. Any left in there?" Hudson asked, pointing to the teapot.

"Yes, should be. Help yourself."

Hudson poured himself a steaming hot cup of tea and desperately tried to resist asking the question that was **lingering** on the tip of his tongue. But it was no use.

"So, have they determined the cause of death?"

"No, not yet. By the looks of the bruising and the position of the body, I'd say it was a **hit-and-run**."

"Yes, quite right…" The inspector could hardly stop himself. He had had the very same thought.

Sergeant Murdoch looked at the inspector in brief **bewilderment** but decided to carry on.

"Anyway, I don't think much will come of the case. No doubt it was an accident, a drunk driver on his way home from the Burns

Supper. Willy was just in the wrong place at the wrong time. He had no family from what we can tell, so I doubt there'll be much call for further investigation."

| | |
|---|---|
| to take sth. at face value | etw. für bare Münze nehmen |
| to be apalled by sth. | über etw. entsetzt sein |
| dereliction of duty | Pflichtversäumnis |

"I hope you don't mind me saying, but that seems awfully unfair," Hudson replied.

Hudson was not only a believer in strong moral values but had also learnt never to take the apparent facts of a death **at face value**.

"Well, that's easily said," Fergus Murdoch answered, a little irritated. "But as far as headquarters are concerned, there's not much more we can do. The heavy snowfall last night covered up any tyre tracks that might have been there. Police work is a complicated business, Mr Hudson, and, to be honest, I think it's something best left to the professionals."

"You're certainly right about that."

Hudson **was appalled by** Fergus' **dereliction of duty**. Was he a lazy worker, or were things really so different here in rural Scotland? Perhaps Fergus was even trying to cover something up… The inspector's imagination began to race.

Hudson couldn't keep his mind off the case. Something didn't feel right to him, and he knew he wouldn't be able to enjoy his holiday until he had found out the truth behind poor Willy's death.

Moments later, he was fully dressed and standing at the reception desk while Dorothy called him a taxi.

"Where did you say you wanted to go to, Mr Hudson?"

"Inverness," the inspector replied. "I have a little business to sort out."

**Exercise 11: True or false?** Welche Aussagen sind korrekt? Markieren Sie mit richtig ✔ oder falsch – !

1. Fergus is aware of Hudson's profession. ☐
2. Dorothy is happy to help her son through difficult times. ☐
3. Fergus shows enthusiasm for solving the case. ☐
4. Hudson is able to put the case to the back of his mind. ☐

After a short wait, the cheery face of Abraham Darling popped out from behind the green front door.
"At your service, Mr Hudson! Didn't think we'd be seeing each other again so soon. I hope last night's misfortune hasn't scared you into going back to London."
"No, not at all, Abraham. Could you take me to the Northern Constabulary headquarters in Longman Road? I have a friend there I'd like to see."
"Your wish is my command. A police officer is he, your friend?"
Hudson could see he wasn't going to be able to hide the truth from Abraham, or any of the other villagers, for much longer.
"Yes, something like that. It's been years since we last saw each other, though."
Abraham thankfully soon stopped asking questions, and the inspector sat back and enjoyed the beautiful Highland scenery speeding past. Fergus had been right about the snow: a good five inches must have fallen overnight.

| Northern Constabulary | Polizei von Nordschottland |
|---|---|

Twenty minutes later they were slowing down outside a modern, red-brick building complex. Hudson entered through the glass doors and stopped to show his police badge at the reception desk.

| | |
|---|---|
| mound | Haufen |
| superintendent | Hauptkommissarin |
| to take a liking to sb. | von jmd. angetan sein |
| tentatively | zögernd |
| to blurt sth. out | etw. ausschwatzen |

"Good morning, Inspector. How can we help?" a young female officer smiled up from behind a towering mound of paperwork.

"I'd like to see Superintendent Akins, please."

"Of course, Inspector. Third floor, room 10. Go on up."

**Exercise 12: Fill in the blanks.** Lesen Sie weiter und vervollständigen Sie den Text!

Unusually for him, Hudson was **1.** *f*_____ a little nervous. He and Hazel Akins had trained together in Scotland Yard when they had both been in their twenties, and the inspector had **2.** *a*_____ **taken** rather **a liking to** the intelligent brunette. He reached her door and **3.** *k*_____ **tentatively**.

"James!" she exclaimed as he entered. "What **4.** *b*_____ you here? It must be fifteen **5.** *y*_____..."

"Hello, Hazel. I'm sorry to call in on you **6.** *l*_____ this," **Hudson blurted out** at **7.** *o*_____.

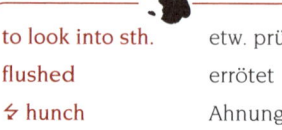

| to look into sth. | etw. prüfen |
|---|---|
| flushed | errötet |
| ⚡ hunch | Ahnung |

"There was a death last night in Glengowan, the village where I'm holidaying. I have reason to believe that it wasn't just an accident, but the police officers in charge aren't overly keen on carrying out an extensive investigation, and…"

Superintendent Akins nodded. She remembered the inspector's strong principles and knew what he was about to ask.

"Yes, James. Go ahead," she said with a knowing smile. "I give you permission to look into the case. I've heard about what that Sergeant Murdoch can be like. It might do him some good to see what a real inspector is capable of."

"Thank you, Hazel," the inspector replied, a little flushed. "I'm sure it's nothing really, but…"

"I know, James. When you have a hunch about a crime, there's no stopping you. I'm afraid I've got a meeting now, but here's my number," she said, pressing a business card into the inspector's hands as she walked out of her office. "Give me a call and let me know how you get along!"

---

**Exercise 13: Word forms.** Ergänzen Sie das jeweilige Substantiv und Adverb!

1. keen _____ _____
2. strong _____ _____
3. know _____ _____
4. sparkling _____ _____

---

The snow was falling heavily as Abraham dropped Hudson off outside the village post office. The little bell above the door rang as he stepped onto the doormat and brushed the snow off his shoes.

| | |
|---|---|
| to be taken aback | aus der Fassung gebracht sein |
| blush | Schamröte |
| plump | füllig |
| shortbread | Buttergebäck |

"Ah, Mr Hudson!" Mavis smiled welcomingly. "Come to buy some postcards already?"

"Hello, Mavis. No, I was wondering if you'd mind me asking a few questions about Willy the bagpiper."

"Why, Mr Hudson! That sounds very formal, anyone would think you were a police officer," Mavis laughed.

"Inspector, actually."

"Oh my." Mavis was clearly taken aback. "I have to say, you do look the type, but… Oh my. Well, we'd best go into the back."

Hudson followed the little lady past the shelves of sweets and envelopes into a small kitchen at the back of the post office.

"Sit yourself down, Mr Hud… Inspector. I'll just pop the kettle on. I couldn't believe my ears this morning when I heard the terrible news. Poor old Willy. Who'd do such a thing?"

"That's exactly what I'd like to find out, Mavis. I've come to you first because, from what I can tell, you seem to know a fair amount about the villagers and what they get up to."

Mavis seemed to take this as a compliment, and a rosy blush spread across her plump cheeks as she pushed a large blue tin across the table to the inspector.

"Have a shortbread, I've just made them."

"Thank you. So, what can you tell me about Willy?" Hudson continued.

"Well, now let me think…" Mavis paused.

"How about starting with Willy's full name, family… Where did he live, for example?" Hudson prompted.

"You know what, Inspector? I know everyone in Glengowan, but Willy was always a mystery to me, I'm afraid."

| ⚡ Scottie dog | Scottish Terrier, brit. Hunderasse |
| ⚡ come rain or shine | bei jedem Wetter |
| passerby | Passant |
| to usher in | hineinführen |

"A mystery in what way?"
"Well, everybody knew of him, of course, but no one really knew much about him. Cheery old Willy the bagpiper and his little Scottie dog. They would sit in the village square every day of the year, come rain or shine. Willy always had a smile and a tune for the passersby, and he collected just enough loose change to get by on. Sometimes I'd bring him out a cup of something hot when it got chilly, but he wasn't one to chat much."
"You don't know where he lived?" the inspector asked again.
"No, I'm afraid not. I never really thought about it, to be honest. Best ask the village mayor, Inspector. He's got a record of those sorts of things."
"Thank you for your help, Mavis. Exceptional shortbread."

**Exercise 14: Antonyms.** Ergänzen Sie das jeweilige Gegenteil!

1. poor old Willy  _____
2. cheery  _____
3. a fair amount  _____
4. plump  _____

It was getting dark as Hudson walked the few metres from the post office to the mayor's house on the far side of the village square.
He pulled the rope of the heavy, old-fashioned doorbell and was immediately ushered in by a smartly-dressed young woman.

"Good afternoon, sir." The secretary gave a stiff smile and went to sit down again behind her desk.

"Inspector Hudson of Scotland Yard. I was wondering if the mayor had a moment to answer a few questions about the events following last night's Burns Supper?"

| intercom | Sprechanlage |
| to crackle | knistern |
| stately | stattlich |
| ornate | kunstvoll |
| etched | geätzt |
| clan | Klan |

The secretary cast the inspector a cold glance. She pressed the buzzer on the small intercom beside her.

"An Inspector Hudson to see you, Mr Cartwright. I can tell him to go away if you're busy…"

"Not at all, Daisy. Send the gentleman in," the mayor's well-spoken voice crackled back through the receiver.

---

**Exercise 15: Unscramble.** Lesen Sie weiter und ordnen Sie die Buchstaben zu sinnvollen Wörtern!

The inspector 1. wolledof _____ Daisy along a stately-looking 2. rocordir _____. The walls were hung with ornate tartan 3. slitaeram _____; below each 4. suarqe _____ drape was a little plaque etched with the name of a Scottish clan.

"Quite an office you've got here, Mayor Cartwright," Hudson said as he entered the 5. isurxluloyu _____ decorated room.

| | |
|---|---|
| ↯ to fill sb. in on sth. | jmd. über etw. informieren |
| French windows *pl* | Fenstertüren |
| to bear with sb. | mit jmd. Geduld haben |
| surly | mürrisch |
| to glower | finster blicken |

"Thank you, Inspector Hudson. A pleasure to make your acquaintance. Please take a seat. How may I be of assistance?"

The inspector sank into a large leather armchair beside the roaring fire.

"I was wondering if you could fill me in on some details about the victim, Willy, who was found dead last night. Name, age, address, that sort of thing."

"Yes, of course. A terrible business. Let me just take a look at the records."

The mayor walked over towards the French windows and bent down over a large wooden filing cabinet.

"We haven't got around to transferring all the files onto a computer yet, so I'm afraid you'll have to bear with me ⓘ while I search through these records… Ah, here we go!"

The mayor returned to the fireplace.

"Mr William MacNorris. Born July 1958 in Glengowan. There's no register of a marriage, and no address given either, I'm afraid."

"Well, it's a start at least," the inspector said gratefully. "I'd best be getting off, but thank you for your time."

Hudson glanced at his watch and hurried to the Loch Inn where Dorothy would no doubt soon be serving her guests a hearty home-cooked dinner. As he reached out a cold hand to turn the brass handle, the door to the hotel was abruptly pulled open.

**Politeness**
Wenn man im Englischen höflich sein möchte, drückt man sich indirekter aus oder entschuldigt sich beispielsweise gleich vorsorglich.

"Good evening, Mr Hudson," the surly, unshaven face of Fergus Murdoch glowered at him from within.

"Or should I call you Inspector?"

**Exercise 16: Word spiral.** Finden Sie die Begriffe in der Wortspirale!

|  1 |  2 |  3 |  4 |  5 |  6 |  7 |  8 |
|----|----|----|----|----|----|----|----|
| 22 | 23 | 24 | 25 | 26 | 27 | 28 |  9 |
| 21 | 36 | 37 | 38 | 39 | 40 | 29 | 10 |
| 20 | 35 | 34 | 33 | 32 | 31 | 30 | 11 |
| 19 | 18 | 17 | 16 | 15 | 14 | 13 | 12 |

- **1-7.** documentation of evidence etc.
- **7-11.** a twisting movement
- **11-18.** lacking vital signs
- **18-21.** frozen water when it is soft and white
- **21-30.** a term describing an eloquent person
- **30-35.** not wide
- **35-40.** a Scottish alcoholic drink

# A Little Knowledge Is a Dangerous Thing

| | |
|---|---|
| chitchat | Geplauder |
| prying | neugierig |

The atmosphere over dinner was more than a little uncomfortable. Dorothy did her best to lift the mood with her good-humoured chitchat, but was unable to compensate for her son's ill temper. After finishing his meal, Hudson rose to help Dorothy with the dishes. Away from the prying ears of the guests, he reached for a tea towel and whispered his apologies to her.
"I didn't mean to lie, Dorothy. The last thing I wanted was to spend my holiday investigating another death, but…"
"Quite alright, Mr Hudson," Dorothy replied in a frosty tone. "Anyway, I think it's my son you ought to be apologizing to."

**Exercise 17: Translation.** Übersetzen Sie folgende Sätze!

1. The atmosphere over dinner was more than a little uncomfortable.

    ___

2. Fergus refused to acknowledge any of the other guests.

    ___

3. Hudson apologized away from the prying ears of the guests.

    ___

Hudson went to find Fergus in the sitting room, where he was **laying the fire**. Hudson poured two glasses of whisky from the decanter on the sideboard and walked towards the **brooding** police sergeant.

| | |
|---|---|
| to lay a fire | ein Feuer anmachen |
| brooding | grüblerisch |
| to humour sb. | jmd. seinen Willen lassen |
| to go back a long way | sich lange kennen |

"I suppose I've got some explaining to do, Sergeant Murdoch..." Hudson waited for Fergus to turn around. "I didn't mean to go behind your back. It's just that I've seen so many mysterious deaths in my time and very rarely have I not been able to solve one. I thought perhaps I could be of some help. Superintendent Akins gave me permission to..."

"Ha! Her again," Fergus interrupted with a cry. "She's never liked me much. I'm sure she was more than happy to make me look the fool."

"Not at all, Sergeant. I think she was just **humouring** an old friend. Hazel and I **go back a long way**."

---

### Exercise 18: Choose the correct alternative. Lesen Sie weiter und unterstreichen Sie die richtige Variante!

"Be that as it **1.** will / may , I would have appreciated it if you could have **2.** informed / reformed me of your intentions before telling **3.** part / half the village."

"I only paid a visit to Mavis and..."

"Mavis is half the village, Inspector. She had telephoned **4.** everywhere / around gossiping to everyone about Dorothy's new guest being from Scotland Yard **5.** after / within seconds of you leaving the post office."

| | |
|---|---|
| busker | Straßenmusikant |
| to file for divorce | die Scheidung einreichen |
| to rummage | wühlen |
| tattered | zerrissen |
| stride | Schritt |

"Well, I really am very sorry. Let's start afresh, shall we?" Hudson held out his hand.

"I would be honoured, Sergeant Murdoch, if you would allow me to help in the investigation of Willy MacNorris' death. I promise to consult you on all proceedings and conform to Northern Constabulary protocol."

Fergus hesitated briefly and shook the inspector's hand.

"Very well. Do what you want. I've not got time to worry about the death of a homeless **busker** anyway. My wife's **filing for divorce** and I've got a mountain of paperwork to get through."

"My sympathies, Sergeant. Perhaps you could give me the case file, that might speed things up a bit."

Fergus nodded and **rummaged** around in his briefcase, which was lying on one of the large, worn-out sofas. He handed Hudson a **tattered** green folder.

"Not much in it, I'm afraid. Just some names and addresses of the people who attended the Burns Supper, and a brief statement taken from Father Angus at the scene of the crime."

"Thank you. I'm sure that's plenty for me to be getting on with for now, Sergeant. Here's to Willy!"

The two men raised their glasses.

"Aye, to Willy."

Early the next morning, the small village of Glengowan lay covered by a thick blanket of fog. From the library window of the rectory, a small, dark figure could be seen walking up the snowy path to the churchyard.

Judging by the figure's assertive **stride**, Father Angus could tell that this was a man on a mission. He wasn't in the least surprised when, a few moments later, the inspector knocked at the front door.

> **Exercise 19: Passive voice.** Formulieren Sie die Sätze im Passiv!
>
> 1. Fergus shook the inspector's hand.
>
> ___
>
> 2. He handed Hudson a green folder.
>
> ___
>
> 3. Father Angus gave a brief statement.
>
> ___
>
> 4. The two men raised their glasses.
>
> ___

"Good morning, Father! I'm sorry to disturb you on a Sunday. May I come in?"
"Morning, Inspector. How may I help you?" Father Angus removed Hudson's wet coat and showed him into the library.
"Ah, I see you've heard."
"Yes, yes. Inspector James Hudson from Scotland Yard. News travels fast, especially with Mavis Leary to speed it along."
"Clearly," Hudson remarked, taking a seat opposite the priest's desk.
"Would you mind me asking a few questions about the events that occurred on Friday the twenty-fifth?"

| key fact | Tatsache |
| begrudgingly | widerwillig |

Father Angus grumbled something to himself and shuffled a few papers around on the desk in front of him.

"Father?" Hudson repeated.

"I gave my statement the night I found the body. I've nothing more to say on the matter."

"I am aware of your existing statement, Father," Hudson said, holding up the case file, "but I'm afraid there are a few **key facts** missing. I'd be very grateful for your help."

"Very well," the Father **begrudgingly** agreed.

---

**Exercise 20: Correct the mistakes.** Lesen Sie weiter und korrigieren Sie die sechs Fehler im folgenden Absatz!

"According to your statement, you found Willy's body at 12:15 p.m. Is that correct?"

"Yes, twenty passed at the latest. Its only a ten-minute walk to the rectory."

"So, Willy must have been killed in the fifteen minutes around you walking to the rectory and back again."

Hudson made a few notes in his folder after carrying on.

"And what about the body. It says here you found him lying face down. Did you recognize anything else?"

1. _____  2. _____

3. _____  4. _____

5. _____  6. _____

"Well, I'm no forensic expert, but it looked as though he'd been hit from behind. His body was lying on the main road but his head must have hit the pavement as he fell, there was so much blood…"

Father Angus was visibly shaken by the memory.

"Thank you, Father, we're almost done. Do you remember anything unusual about Willy's behaviour during the Burns Supper?"

"I didn't know him very well, Inspector, so I'm afraid it's hard for me to say, but now I think about it, it is rather odd… I could have sworn I saw Willy leaving the supper just before eleven. He wasn't one for parties, and I remember being surprised that he stayed so long at all. I wonder what he was doing outside in the cold until midnight."

"Did you see anyone leaving with him?"

"Not that I can remember. He said goodbye to Mayor Cartwright and his wife and left through the foyer. Always kept himself to himself."

"Well, you've been most helpful, Father," Hudson said, getting up to leave. "Just one more question: do you own a car?"

"No, Inspector. I've no need for one. I rarely leave the parish, and if I do, Mrs MacDougal is usually happy to give me a lift."

"Mrs MacDougal?"

"Yes, Morag. Duncan's wife. We sat next to Duncan at the Burns Supper. He runs the Glengowan wool mill."

"Ah, yes. I remember now. And where was Mrs MacDougal that night? I don't recall meeting her."

"I'm not one to pry into other people's business, Inspector. Perhaps you'd better ask her yourself."

Hudson unhooked his coat from the stand and walked to the door.

"Right. Well, thank you for your time, Father. I'll see myself out."

**Exercise 21: Questions about the text.** Beantworten Sie die Fragen zum Text!

1. What was Willy's attitude to public festivities?

   _____

2. Would you describe the bagpiper as outgoing?

   _____

3. Why does Father Angus not need to own a car?

   _____

4. To what extent does the priest interest himself in the business of others?

   _____

As Hudson left the rectory, he pulled out his mobile phone from his coat pocket. He hadn't turned it on since arriving, in the hope of not being disturbed, but that was clearly no longer an option. The phone immediately vibrated with a series of messages notifying him of his missed calls.

"Ah, Miss Paddington," Hudson said out loud to himself, "been missing me already, have you?"
He dialled and waited.

| scrapyard | Schrottplatz |

"Sergeant Murdoch speaking."
"Fergus, I hope I'm not disturbing you. I was wondering if you could do me a favour and check out the local car garages and scrapyards to see if they've had any cars in since Friday that

show signs of being involved in a hit-and-run."

"One step ahead of you, Inspector. I'm on my way as we speak. Meet me at The Bagpiper's Arms at six-thirty, I'll fill you in on the details."

| | |
|---|---|
| ↯ Nessie | Spitzname für das Loch Ness Monster |
| awning | Markise |
| keepsake | Andenken |
| cluttered | vollgestellt |
| novelty | *hier*: Kuriosität |

"Good work, Sergeant. Just one more thing: who's carrying out the autopsy on Willy's body? I can't seem to find a name."

"Dr Conall, the best pathologist this side of Edinburgh. I told her to get in touch with you as soon as the results come through tomorrow morning."

"Wonderful, we're not such a bad team after all!"

Fergus was silent.

"Well, see you later."

On his way to Glengowan wool mill, Hudson passed a small souvenir shop with "Nessie Nostalgia" written in large letters across an orange awning.

I ought to get a little keepsake for Miss Paddington, the inspector thought to himself as he peered through the cluttered shop window. She'll be disappointed if I come home empty-handed.

Hudson opened the creaky shop door and was overwhelmed by the sheer mass of Loch Ness Monster-related memorabilia. Hundreds if not thousands of Nessie replicas of all colours,

**Das Loch Ness Monster**
Die Existenz von „Nessie", zuerst 1934 gesichtet, konnte nie bewiesen werden. Allein 2007 brachte Nessie dem schottischen Tourismus aber geschätzte 6 Mio. Pfund ein.

shapes and sizes lined the crammed shelves. On the other side of the room were seemingly endless piles of Nessie posters, mugs, wind-up toys and other useless novelties.

**Exercise 22: If-clauses.** Bringen Sie die Wörter in die richtige Reihenfolge, um if-Sätze zu bilden!

1. mobile | been | have | would | on | Hudson | if | had | he | his | left | disturbed

2. wants | more | must | Fergus | Hudson | if | pub | to | the | at | meet | he | know

3. results | contact | the | she | if | will | pathologist | any | has | Hudson

4. be | may | Miss Paddington | returns | if | empty-handed | disappointed | home | Hudson

"Quite a collection you've got here!" Hudson remarked to the **sturdy** man behind the **till**.

The shopkeeper wore a red tartan cap and a black T-shirt with "I BELIEVE" written in large red capitals across the chest.

"Thank you," the man smiled back with a semi-toothless grin.

"Looking for something to take back to the wife?"

"Something like that, yes."

He reached for a green Nessie **oven mitt** and matching apron set.

| | |
|---|---|
| sturdy | kräftig |
| till | Kasse |
| oven mitt | Topflappen |

"This will do nicely."

"An Englishman, aye? Don't suppose you're that Inspector Rudson they all keep talking about?" the shopkeeper asked.

"Hudson. Yes, that's me."

| | |
|---|---|
| vigorous | energisch |
| disheartened | entmutigt |
| penchant | Vorliebe |
| each to his own | jedem das Seine |
| windy | *hier*: kurvenreich |

"John Murray," the man said, giving Hudson a **vigorous** handshake. "Pleased to make your acquaintance. I hear you're looking into Friday's mishap? Terrible business, that."

"Yes, quite."

Hudson passed him a twenty-pound note before continuing, "I don't suppose you can tell me anything about Mr MacNorris that might be of use to our investigation?"

"About Willy? Nothing that I can think of."

"Yes, that seems to be everybody's answer," Hudson replied, a little **disheartened**.

"He was a quiet man, you see, Inspector. Always polite but never had much to say for himself."

John handed Hudson some change and folded his large, muscular arms across his chest.

"Seemed to have a bit of a **penchant** for Nessie memorabilia, though," John chuckled.

"How do you mean?"

"Well, every so often, when he had a penny to spare after busking, he'd come and buy a little keepsake of some sort. Usually a figurine or the latest copy of Nessie News."

"**Each to his own**, I suppose," the inspector said with a smile. "Perhaps he bought them for his children?"

"No, Willy didn't have any children. I remember asking him the very same question myself. Just his little dog Hamish. I used to see them walking home together every night, down that lane there," he pointed out the window to a narrow, **windy** path.

| | |
|---|---|
| wee (Scot) | klein |
| ⚡ mite | Armer |
| to keep one's eyes peeled | die Augen offen halten |

"Is that so?" Hudson was growing curious. "Do you know where Willy lived, then?"
"No, but it can't be far from here. The lane's only half a mile long, it leads down to Loch Ness. So who's taking care of little Hamish?"
"I'm afraid that thought hadn't occurred to me…"
"Oh, the **wee mite**! He'll be half-starved by now, wherever he is."
But Hudson had stopped listening and was making a mental note to take a trip down the lane as soon as he'd cleared up a few unanswered questions with Mrs MacDougal.
"Well, thanks for the apron, Mr Murray." Hudson turned to leave.
"My pleasure, Inspector. Come back any time!"

**Exercise 23: Prepositions.** Lesen Sie weiter und ergänzen Sie den Text mit den Präpositionen!

As soon as John Murray saw Hudson's figure disappear 1. _____ the foggy road, he sprang up 2. _____ behind the till. Grabbing his coat and a packet of Nessie dog food from one of the shelves, he jolted 3. _____ of the shop. The door shut 4. _____ him with a bang, and a handwritten sign reading "Back in 10" was left swinging 5. _____ the handle.

John walked quickly down the windy path, **keeping his eyes peeled** for any signs of a house. After a few minutes, he'd reached the end of the track and was standing on a muddy red shore, staring right out at Loch Ness.

"What a view!" he shouted out in awe.

A fine mist **hovered** above the blue-grey water, and the

| to hover | in der Luft schweben |
| yapping | Kläffen |
| to placate sb. | jmd. besänftigen |
| ↯ nosh | Fressalien |
| grime | Schmutz |
| to obliterate | verdecken |
| ↯ poky | winzig |

wide panorama was as beautiful as any John had ever seen. In the distance he could make out what looked like a little fishing hut and, as he drew closer, he heard the unmistakable barking of a dog.

"Hamish?"

His call was answered by louder, more excited **yapping**. The door to the hut was locked, but one pull of the padlock and it immediately snapped off in John's strong hands. Hamish jumped at him, wagging his little white tail.

"There's a good boy, Hamish. You poor little…."

John suddenly stopped in his tracks. As his eyes adjusted to the darkness in the hut, he began to see that the walls around him were plastered in newspaper clippings. Not a single inch had been spared. Creeping closer, he brushed the dust and cobwebs aside with his sleeve and began to read. Each one was, without exception, about the Loch Ness Monster. John knew that Willy had been a bit of a fanatic, but this was unthinkable.

After fishing through the mountain of newspapers on the floor, John found Hamish's dog bowl and **placated** the terrier's whimpering with a big helping of Nessie **Nosh**. A thick layer of dust and **grime** almost entirely **obliterated** the view through the **poky** window, with the exception of a small circle in the middle, which had been wiped clean. John's gaze strayed to the old, battered table beneath the window. A pair of binoculars lay beside a

| scrawl | Gekrakel |
| snug | gemütlich, kuschelig |
| skein | Strang |
| loom | Webmaschine |

thick, yellowing notebook. He squinted in the dim light, trying to make sense of Willy's childish **scrawl**.

Suddenly, a strong wind whistled through the timber shack and John felt the hairs on his neck stand on end. Without warning, he leapt up from where he had been kneeling, ripped a handful of pages from the book and raced out the door as fast as his legs could carry him.

Meanwhile, Inspector Hudson was sitting comfortably in Morag MacDougal's **snug** workshop, watching her unravel a large, round **skein** of wool. The **looms** clicked gently in the background as Hudson posed one question after the other.

"Judging by the guest list, Mrs MacDougal, you had never intended to take part in the Burns Night celebrations."

"No, Inspector," she looked up at him through a tangle of brown wool. "My father is very ill, and I promised to spend the evening with him and my mother at their home in Huntly. It's over on the other side of the loch, about a twenty-minute drive from here."

"Until what time did you stay with your parents?"

"I'm not sure exactly. I must have left around 11:40 p.m. I remember picking Duncan up from the village hall just as the church bells chimed midnight."

"And then you both drove straight home?"

"Yes."

"You didn't come across anything suspicious? A car speeding off, a dead body lying on the roadside?"

"No, Inspector. I'm sure I would have remembered something as gruesome as that."

"Had you been drinking?"

Morag looked down at her round, protruding belly.

"Yes, of course not, my mistake," the inspector apologized. "Well, I suppose that's it for now. May I speak to your husband?"
"He's **herding in** the sheep. You'll probably find him down by the little stream in the east field."
"Thank you, Mrs MacDougal. You take care of yourself now."
Hudson walked down the stone steps and out onto the frosty field. The grass crunched loudly

| | |
|---|---|
| to herd in | hüten |
| flock | Herde |
| incessant | ununterbrochen |
| bleating | Geblöke |

beneath his feet as he walked towards Duncan MacDougal, who was standing amidst his **flock** of sheep.

---

**Exercise 24: Translation quiz.** Übersetzen Sie und enträtseln Sie das Lösungswort!

1. jdn. beruhigen
2. verdecken
3. knirschen
4. läuten
5. entwirren
6. grausig
7. eindeutig
8. Strang

Lösung: ☐☐☐☐☐☐☐☐

---

"Good afternoon, Mr Hudson!" Duncan shouted out over the **incessant bleating**. "Don't be afraid, they'll do you no harm!"

| | |
|---|---|
| to beckon | jmd. heranwinken |
| staff | *hier*: Stock |
| bedraggled | ungepflegt |
| snarl | Zähnefletschen |
| detour | Umleitung |

He **beckoned** with his **staff** for Hudson to come closer.

"I won't keep you long, Mr MacDougal," Hudson said, a little out of breath.

"I've just been speaking to your wife. Could you tell me what time you left the Burns Supper on Friday?"

"Aye, must have been midnight. I wanted to be in bed by half twelve because I had to get up early on Saturday to let out the sheep."

"And I suppose you didn't see anything suspicious either?"

"Not on the way home, Inspector, no. But I do remember hearing a woman sobbing in the cloakroom as I left the village hall."

"Do carry on."

"I didn't stop to see who it was. I didn't want to keep Morag waiting outside in the cold, not in her condition."

"Yes, of course."

From the corner of his eye, Hudson saw a **bedraggled** brown sheep approaching with a **snarl**.

"Well, you've been most helpful. I'd best be getting on."

Hudson made a hasty exit back to the safety of the mill. Before leaving, he made a short **detour** across the front lawn and slipped into the garage at the side of the main house. Mrs MacDougal's little blue car seemed to be in good condition, with no bumps or scratches that would suggest any sort of collision.

It was dark as Hudson walked back towards the centre of the village. Fergus would be waiting and there was no time for his expedition to Willy's hut.

It'll have to wait until tomorrow, Hudson thought as he looked at his watch and stepped into the warm glow of the pub.

#  Follow my Footsteps

A strong wind rattled against the small, rickety windows of The Bagpiper's Arms. Safely inside, Fergus was already onto his third pint while Hudson nestled a tumbler of whisky in the palm of his hand.

"So there's not been a single car within a fifty-mile radius that's been brought into a garage for repairs or respraying since Friday?"

"Aye, well not quite. There were two in Dunfirth and another three in Kilmuir, but none of them had any damage specific to the rear or bonnet. The mechanic at MacFix said that if the body didn't hit the windscreen on impact, there might not have been much damage."

Hudson was disappointed by Fergus' findings.

"And what about the scrapyards?"

"Two cars were scrapped on Saturday morning in Inverness."

"That sounds promising."

"The scrapping company is going to fax me the names of the owners first thing tomorrow and then I'll pay them a visit."

| rickety | klapprig |
| bonnet | Motorhaube |
| blizzard | Schneesturm |

"Very well. Better not drink any more of those, then," Hudson said, pointing to Fergus' empty pint glass.

"Aye, Inspector," Fergus complied with a wink, "let's be leaving then." The two men fought their way home through the blizzard, while the inspector filled Fergus in on his latest findings.

**Exercise 25: Fill in the blanks.** Lesen Sie weiter und setzen Sie die Ausdrücke in der korrekten Form ein!

| echo | to stop oneself | find out | wait for | walk up |
| silent |

Meanwhile, John Murray was also back in Glengowan. Angry and confused by his discovery, the ever-conscientious shopkeeper hadn't been able **1.** _____ from **2.** _____ more. Now, standing in the icy darkness, he crushed the pages of Willy's diary in his large fists and waited.

It was some time before a figure came **3.** _____ the driveway and unlocked the entrance. He followed **4.** _____ and slipped into the house before the door shut behind him with an **5.** _____ bang. As the figure turned to face him, however, John realized that it wasn't the person he had been **6.** _____.

"What are you doing here?" the cold voice cut into the silence.
"I-I-I was looking for...," John stammered, losing his nerve.
He could tell that events were not about to go as planned.
"What have you got there?"
Alarmed by the threatening tone, John hesitantly **proffered** the scrunched-up papers, but immediately regretted his decision.

| to proffer | anbieten |

The yelling and cursing that **ensued** could be heard all through the house, if only someone had been there to listen.

"I'm sorry, I think there's been some sort of misunderstanding. I didn't mean…"

| | |
|---|---|
| to ensue | folgen |
| to slump | sacken, fallen |
| cinder | Asche |
| to consume | *hier*: verzehren |
| insufferable | unerträglich |
| racket | Lärm |

John wanted nothing more than to leave; his heart pounded violently and the words choked him as he tried to speak. But before he could reach the door, he felt a cold rush of wind along his neck, followed instantaneously by an almighty crack against his skull.

John's body **slumped** to the floor. Through his half-opened eyes, he could just make out the blurred figure throw the crumpled pages furiously into the glowing **cinders** of the fireplace beside him.

Paralyzed by pain, he watched as the words were **consumed** by the flames before closing his eyes for the very last time.

Hudson had been sleeping peacefully under the woolly covers of his four-poster bed when he was woken by a high-pitched ringing.

"What an **insufferable racket**," he grumbled as his hand felt sleepily around the bedside table for the cause of the commotion.

He lifted the heavy, old-fashioned receiver to his ear.

"Hudson speaking," he croaked, sitting himself up in bed.

"I'm sorry to wake you so early, James."

It was the pleasantly familiar voice of Hazel Akins.

"No, no, not at all. I was just…" Hudson looked at his alarm clock: six-thirty.

"…about to get up. To what do I owe the pleasure?"

"A body has been found by some workers at a dump a few miles from Glengowan. I thought I ought to let you know."

"Yes, thank you."

"I've already spoken to Sergeant Murdoch and…"

| | |
|---|---|
| dump | Müllhalde |
| skip | Schuttcontainer |

At that moment, there was a knock at the inspector's door. Fergus quietly called out the inspector's name.

"Speak of the devil! We'll get on to it right away, Hazel."

### Exercise 26: What would have happened?
**Vervollständigen Sie die if-Sätze!**

1. If John hadn't been so alarmed, he wouldn't have

   _____

2. If someone else had been in the house, they

   _____

3. John might have been able to save the papers, had

   _____

4. _____

   if the telephone hadn't rung.

A few moments later, the two men were speeding down the steep Highland streets in Fergus' little police car. Dawn hadn't yet broken as they approached Munlochy rubbish dump. Beneath the floodlights, they could see a crowd of people gathering around one of the large orange skips.

While Fergus went to speak to the police officers on duty, Hudson pushed his way through the onlookers and peered down into the container. Lying amidst a mountain of bulging black **bin-liners**, the inspector could make out two muddy boots poking out from a bundle of tartan cloth.

| | |
|---|---|
| bin-liner | Müllbeutel |
| stretcher | Krankenbahre |
| endearing | reizend |

"Mind your head, sir!"

Two young officers lifted a **stretcher** over the side of the container and hauled the lifeless body out from the garbage and into the shelter of the sterile, white tent that had been erected a few metres from the skip.

"Here you go, Dr Conall. He's all yours," they said, setting the body down on a large plastic sheet.

Hudson watched the young woman in her white overalls as she thanked the two officers. Her blonde hair was tied back in a messy bun and her thick spectacles magnified her sleepy green eyes in an unflattering but curiously **endearing** way.

"Hello, Dr Conall," Hudson called, walking towards her. "Inspector Hudson from Scotland Yard."

"Ah! Inspector Hudson!" she flashed him a wide, friendly smile. "Cordelia Conall, an honour to meet you."

Hudson stepped to one side as she began to unravel the body from the bloodstained cloth.

"Oh... good Lord!" Hudson exclaimed.

Dr Conall carefully wiped the blood from the victim's face as she searched for the wound. She looked up at Hudson's pale face.

"What is it, Inspector?"

"That's the man... That's... John. John Murray..."

Hudson's voice trailed off as he watched Cordelia roll John's body over. He was still wearing the same black T-shirt that Hudson had seen him in the previous afternoon.

"Look at this, Inspector."

**Exercise 27: Translation.** Lesen Sie weiter und fügen Sie die Übersetzung der angegebenen Begriffe richtig ein!

| zur Leichenhalle | ich würde sagen | umzirkeln |
| durch einen Schlag | Kopf schüttelnd | Zeitpunkt |
| zeigen auf | zum jetzigen |

She **1.** a long **gash** on the back of John's head.
"At a **cursory** glance, **2.** he was killed **3.** to the head, and a nasty one at that."
"I'm beginning to wish I'd stayed at home," Hudson said, **4.** .
He **5.** the body lying in the middle of the tent and **prodded** the brown and red tartan cloth beside it.
"I'm going to take him down **6.** now, Inspector. I'm afraid there's not much more I can tell you **7.** ."

| gash | Schnittwunde |
| cursory | kursorisch |
| to prod | stupsen |

"Could you spare me a corner of this material here, Dr Conall? A few inches would be fine."
"I shouldn't really, not until I've run a few tests."

Cordelia glanced at Hudson, who looked tired and a little **despondent** after the morning's events. Suddenly she felt sorry for the kind-hearted Englishman.

| | |
|---|---|
| despondent | mutlos |
| ⚡ to plop down | hinplumpsen |
| rundown | Zusammenfassung |

"Oh, go on then."
She ripped off a piece and stuffed it into the inspector's pocket. "But don't tell anyone it was me who gave it to you!" she told him.
"Excuse me, Inspector," Fergus suddenly peered in through the tent. "The men are eager to get back to work. The sooner we get the questioning over and done with, the sooner they can carry on with their bin rounds."
"Yes, of course, Sergeant," Hudson replied, following Fergus out to a small group of men dressed in fluorescent yellow vests.
"Good morning, gentlemen. Which of you found the body, then?"
The shortest of the four bin men raised his hand.
"Me, Sir. Brian Milne."
"Right, you come with me. Sergeant Murdoch here will take care of the rest of you."
Hudson led the round little man to the workers' cabin on the far side of the dump.
"Mind if we step inside here for a few minutes, Mr Milne?" he asked.
"Make yourself at home, Inspector," Brian nodded and gestured to a grimy armchair by the door.
"I think I'll stand, thank you."
"As you wish," Brian sighed, and **plopped down** on it.

> Titel und Berufsbezeichnungen wie **Inspector** werden im Englischen nur großgeschrieben, wenn es sich um eine direkte Anrede handelt oder sie als Teil eines Namens verwendet werden, z. B. **Inspector Hudson**. In allen anderen Fällen werden sie kleingeschrieben.

"How about giving me a brief **rundown**?"

**Exercise 28: Synonyms.** Lesen Sie weiter und unterstreichen Sie die Entsprechungen zu den folgenden Begriffen!

`waste container`  `unguarded`  `stinking`  `except`  `to smile`

"Aye, well... I came down to the dump this morning, five o'clock as usual. Billy and Kenneth were already preparing the lorry – Mondays is when we collect the bins in Huntly – and I went to see if any of the skips needed emptying before we left. Sometimes they get full over the weekend with people bringing down things they don't want."
"So the dump is left unattended at weekends?"
"Aye, no need to supervise a smelly mound of rubbish, is there, Inspector? No one would want to steal it, apart from the crows."
"Then I don't suppose you have any CCTV cameras here?"
"Ah, but that we do have, Inspector!"
Brian beamed proudly and pointed to a small camera in the corner of the ceiling.

"It looks out over to where the rubbish lorries are parked. We lock them up behind that gate there, but the insurance company explicitly stipulated surveillance cameras as well."

| | |
|---|---|
| CCTV camera | Videoüberwachungssystem |
| to beam | strahlen |
| to stipulate | vertraglich festsetzen |

"That's something at least. Would you mind giving Sergeant Murdoch the tape when we've finished here?"
Brian nodded.

| | |
|---|---|
| ⚡ to be in good nick | top in Schuss sein |
| rap | *hier*: Klopfen |

"Right, and so that was when you found the body?"
"Yes, must have been about quarter to six by the time I got round to that last skip. I noticed a pair of muddy boots that were still in quite good nick and reached down to pick them up. That's when I realized they were still being worn. Wouldn't have noticed the body otherwise, all wrapped up and with a few bin bags thrown over to cover it up."
"But other than that you didn't notice anything else suspicious this morning?"
"I don't think so," Brian said with a yawn.
"Well, don't hesitate to call if…"
Hudson was interrupted by a loud rap on the cabin door.
"Inspector?" Fergus' voice bellowed with some urgency. "Could you step out here for a moment, sir."
Hudson opened the rusty metal door. "What is it, Sergeant? I'm…"
Fergus stood in the yellow light of the cabin window holding a battered set of bagpipes. Hudson tried to suppress a smile.
"I hope that's what I think it is, Fergus."
"One of the officers found them in the same skip as the body. I'm fairly certain they belong to Willy."
"Well, what are you waiting for? Give them to Dr Conall for analysis. It looks like we've got a serial murderer on our hands…"
"I'm afraid Dr Conall has already left, Inspector. I'll drive them to her lab right away."
"I need you to come to the wool mill with me first, though. Perhaps send a few of your officers along as well."
"Got a lead, have you?"

to scurry — trippeln

"The material that John's body was wrapped in looks familiar. And until Dr Conall can tell us more, it's all we've got to go on."

"You've a fine eye for detail," Fergus gave Hudson a heavy pat on the back as they walked towards the car. "I have to say, sir, I'm glad you're here. Glengowan has never seen the likes of this and, to be honest, it's nice to have someone around who knows what they're doing."

Hudson smiled faintly at the compliment.

### Exercise 29: Reported speech. Verwandeln Sie die Sätze in die indirekte Rede!

1. "Could you step out here for a moment, sir?" Fergus bellowed.

   _____

2. "What is it, Sergeant?" Hudson demanded.

   _____

3. "It looks like we've got a serial murderer on our hands," Hudson speculated.

   _____

4. "I need you to come with me to the wool mill first," the inspector requested.

   _____

Morag MacDougal's face dropped as she saw the police officers gathering outside her kitchen window. She **scurried** out into the snowy garden, waving her yellow dishcloth in the air.

"Inspector Hudson?" she called from across the lawn.

outhouse     Nebengebäude

"Now, now, Mrs MacDougal," he reassured her, placing an arm around the heavily-pregnant woman.

He led her back into the warmth of the mill, explaining as they walked about John's death and the tartan material.

"I-I see, Inspector," she stuttered. "Well, please go ahead and search the storage rooms."

**Exercise 30: Translation.** Lesen Sie weiter und übersetzen Sie die folgenden Sätze ins Deutsche!

Hudson nodded a go-ahead to Sergeant Murdoch and tore off a piece of the tartan cloth for him. The police officers immediately headed towards the **outhouse**, where all the rolls of material were stored.

"Though I can tell you now," Morag continued, rubbing the brown tartan between her fingers, "you won't find anything like this in our mill."

"And why would that be?" Hudson asked sceptically.

| | |
|---|---|
| A&E (Accident & Emergency) | Notaufnahme |
| ⚡ peck | flüchtiger Kuss |

"It's too soft for sheep's wool. Probably llama. And the tartan isn't a pattern that we produce down here. The lines are too narrow and the colours too pale."

"I'm not quite sure I follow, Mrs MacDougal."

"You see, Inspector," Morag explained, "in the old days, every Scottish clan used to design their own tartan, so you could immediately tell who they were and where they came from. The colours and styles vary from district to district and the tartans around here are bolder, with thicker lines. This looks like it comes from further north."

At that moment, Fergus walked into the kitchen.

"Nothing, Inspector," he said shaking his head. "We couldn't even find anything that looked vaguely similar."

"Right, well, that's all for now, Mrs MacDougal. Thank you again for your cooperation. I'll make sure the officers clear up after themselves. And just for procedure's sake… where were you and your husband between yesterday afternoon and early this morning?"

"At the hospital, Inspector," Duncan's deep voice thundered through the room as he walked in through the back door. "My wife had stomach cramps after dinner and we paid a visit to A&E in Inverness to make sure there was nothing wrong with the baby. They kept her in for observation until eight o'clock this morning, and I was with her the whole time, wasn't I, darling?"

Duncan rubbed Morag's round stomach and gave her a quick peck on the cheek. She smiled up at her husband and confirmed their alibi.

"Well, I hope you're feeling better now, Mrs MacDougal," Hudson said, ushering Fergus out the door. "We're sorry to have bothered you."

"What do you make of that then, Inspector?" Fergus asked eagerly as they walked away from the mill. "I reckon Duncan was lying."

"Oh, I don't think so, Fergus. He's just a little overprotective of his wife. But not to worry, I've got another idea. Though I think I'll deal with this next one by myself."

Hudson left Fergus with a few orders before **trudging** back through the snow to the village square.

---

**Exercise 31: Plural.** Bilden Sie die richtige Pluralform!

1. The woman's round stomach.

   _____

2. He kept her in for observation.

   _____

3. The policeman's car.

   _____

4. The tartan's colour varies.

   _____

---

Daisy's unfriendly face greeted the inspector as he pushed open the door to the mayor's office.

"Wipe your feet, please," she snapped.

Hudson was acquainted with Daisy's **inhospitality** and didn't let it **perturb** him.

| to trudge | mit schweren Schritten gehen |
| inhospitality | Unwirtlichkeit |
| to perturb sb. | jmd. beunruhigen |

"I'd like to see Mayor Cartwright, please."

| | |
|---|---|
| to instil sth. into sb. | jmd. etw. anerziehen |
| spiteful | boshaft |
| to bleach | ausbleichen |
| to distract sb. | jmd. ablenken |
| charred | verkohlt |
| brisk | flott |

He held out his police badge in the hope of **instilling** some respect in the **spiteful** secretary.

"He's not here," she barked. "You'll have to come back tomorrow."

"I'm afraid it can't wait. I was hoping to have a quick look at the tartan hangings in the hallway. I'm sure the mayor wouldn't mind."

Before Daisy could stop him, the inspector had slipped past her desk and into the long hallway. The hangings were all intact, just as Hudson had remembered them, but as he reached the end of the hall, he noticed one that looked newer than the others. It had clearly just been put up and had not yet been **bleached** by the sunlight streaming in through the windows opposite. Hudson made a note of the name of the clan inscribed on the plaque below.

"Caithness. Now we're getting somewhere."

Daisy was meanwhile **distracted** by a telephone call, and Hudson used the opportunity to slip unnoticed into the mayor's office.

The French doors had been left open, and a strong breeze blew in across the fireplace, unsettling the ashes. A corner of **charred** paper caught the inspector's eye and he bent down to retrieve it from the coals. As he did so, he noticed a red, muddy footprint on the beige carpet. Taking a step back, he saw another... and another.

All of a sudden, he heard women's voices approaching the office. He carefully collected the remains of the papers from the fireplace and made a **brisk** exit through the French doors and into the garden. A few moments later, Hudson was back in the safety of the village square.

**Exercise 32: Crossword puzzle.** Lösen Sie das Kreuzworträtsel!

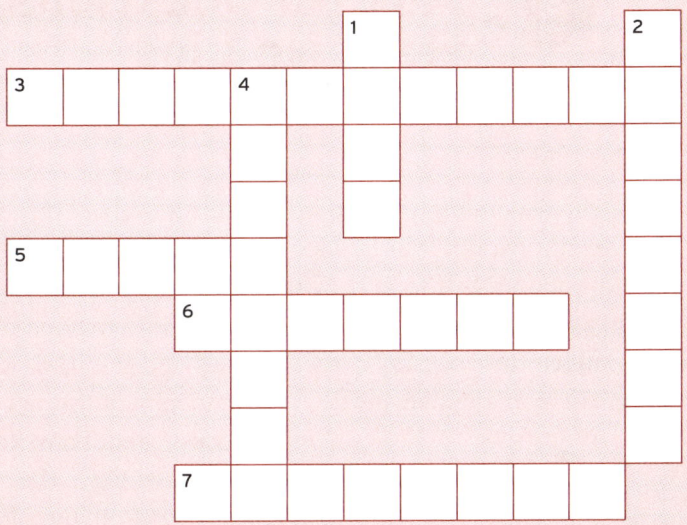

### Across

3. unfriendly and unwelcoming

5. upright

6. to alarm or worry

7. in a tired manner

### Down

1. measure of beer

2. automotive engineer

4. showing malice

# 5. Ask No Questions, Hear No Lies

Darkness was beginning to creep in as Hudson walked through the village graveyard towards Glengowan police station. The stone-clad building at the end of the shadowy lane was little more than a ramshackle cottage. A blue police lantern hung **precariously** above the door, its glass smashed and the light bulb flickering. Hudson stepped inside. The simplicity of the rickety wooden desks and bare linoleum flooring peeling at the corners was a far cry from the **plush** interiors of Scotland Yard.

| | |
|---|---|
| precariously | unsicher |
| plush | nobel |
| pensive | nachdenklich |
| ↯ a few bob | ziemlich viel Geld |

Fergus sat behind a red desk lamp at the furthest table. Hudson walked over and pulled up a chair.

"Hello Sergeant," Hudson greeted the **pensive** officer.

"Aye, Inspector," Fergus looked up, shielding his eyes from the glare of the lamp. "Want to tell me what you've been up to?"

"All in good time, Fergus," Hudson answered. "Did you get any further with researching the material found on John's body?"

"The only llama farm I could find in northern Scotland is in a village near Caithness, about a hundred miles from here, right on the North Sea coast. You can order their tartan online; it costs **a few bob** but they make the cloth we're looking for."

"Caithness!" Hudson beamed. "Fantastic, we're getting closer Fergus, I'm sure of it."

**Exercise 33: Synonyms.** Lesen Sie weiter und unterstreichen Sie die Entsprechungen zu folgenden Wörtern!

correspond to   suspicious   discovered   expressionlessly

Fergus forced a smile, unsure as to why the inspector was so euphoric.

"I need you to get me a **search warrant** for the mayor's house. There's something very fishy going on there."

"The mayor's house? Is that really necessary, Inspector?"

"I took the liberty of searching the mayor's office and found traces of red footprints that match the mud on John's boots. And I'm certain that the material with which the body was wrapped came from there as well. I want you to call in a forensics team and check for evidence of John's murder."

Fergus had turned pale. He looked blankly at the inspector.

"Cheer up," Hudson said loudly. "We've got our murder scene, now we just need to find the murderer…"

search warrant — Durchsuchungsbefehl

| | |
|---|---|
| piqued | pikiert |
| fuzzy | unscharf |
| food for thought | Stoff zum Nachdenken |
| backlog | Arbeitsrückstand |

Fergus nodded silently.

"Well, just get me the warrant."

Hudson was a little **piqued** by Fergus' lack of enthusiasm.

"Have you had a look at the CCTV footage from Munlochy rubbish dump?" he asked more brightly, trying to lift the mood.

Fergus turned his bulky computer monitor around to face the inspector and fast-forwarded the **fuzzy** black and white footage.

"Most of it's just like this," Fergus remarked, pointing to the still, lifeless images of the rubbish lorries. "But here, at 2:42 a.m.…"

They watched a dark, hooded figure walk across the screen.

"What are they doing?" Hudson asked, trying to make out the blurred movements.

"I think they're looking for something. You see, they walk from one skip to the next and then pull out what looks like a large cardboard box from one of them."

Hudson rewound the tape for a second look.

"Then they walk back towards the entrance of the dump and out of sight of the camera," Fergus continued. "And that's it until the bin men start work again at 4:48 a.m."

"I can't even make out if it's a man or a woman. Well, it's **food for thought**, eh? I'd best be getting back, I've got an early start tomorrow."

"You go on ahead, Inspector. I've got to get through this **backlog** first," Fergus grumbled, pointing to the files beside him.

> Da das Geschlecht der Person hier unbekannt ist, wird das neutrale **they** anstatt „he" oder „she" verwendet.

"Very well, Sergeant. Thank you for all your effort."

Hudson nodded goodnight and walked back out into the snowy darkness.

**Exercise 34: Verb forms.** Lesen Sie weiter und ergänzen Sie die richtige Verbform!

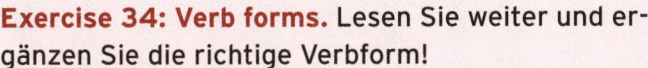

help oneself   can   be   step   be ready   be
be due

Hudson **1.** _____ smell the coffee brewing as he **2.** _____ out of his bedroom the next morning and tiptoed down the creaky wooden stairs of the Loch Inn. Abraham **3.** _____ to pick him up in half an hour.

"Good morning, Dorothy," he said, sitting himself down at the dining table. He **4.** _____ the only guest in the room.

"**5.** _____ to coffee, Mr Hudson," she replied in her usual **bubbly** voice. "The **porridge 6.** _____ in a minute."

"Delicious, thank you. **7.** _____ Fergus up yet?"

"To be honest, I don't think he even went to bed. The lights in the study were on all night and I could hear him **squabbling** on the phone; probably Jessie, his wife. It's a messy busi-

bubbly        quirlig
porridge      Haferbrei
to squabble   zanken

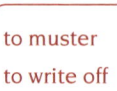

| to muster | zusammenbringen |
| to write off | als Totalschaden deklarieren |

ness, divorce. Breaks my heart to see him like this."

"To see who like what?"

At that moment, Fergus walked into the dining room, still wearing his creased uniform from the day before.

"Ah, Fergus! Just the man I wanted to see," Hudson said, **mustering** as much good cheer as he could.

"Before I leave, is there any news on the scrapped cars yet?" Fergus yawned and poured himself a large mug of coffee.

"Aye, the one car was owned by a Mr Ryan. His car was **written off** after an accident last Wednesday and he's got the police reports to prove it."

"And the other?"

"Errr, well…"

---

**Exercise 35: Idiomatic expressions.** Schreiben Sie die Sätze mit Wendungen aus dem obigen Abschnitt neu!

1. Divorce is a **complicated matter.**

   _____

2. You're **exactly who I** was looking for!

   _____

3. He smiled **as enthusiastically as possible.**

   _____

4. **How come** you didn't let me know?

   _____

"Yes?" Hudson prompted impatiently, checking his watch.

"Apparently, sir, the other car belongs to my wife."

"Christ, you do know how to make things complicated, Fergus. Why on earth didn't you tell me…"

Hudson was interrupted by the doorbell.

"Damn. That'll be Abraham. Call me when you've got the warrant for the mayor's house," Hudson called out, slamming the door behind him. "And as for your wife, she'd better have a good explanation or I'm taking you off the case altogether."

Hudson's mood was little better by the time Abraham dropped him off outside the police headquarters in Inverness thirty minutes later.

Dr Conall welcomed the inspector into her **impeccably** shiny laboratory.

| | |
|---|---|
| impeccably | makellos |
| indentation | Vertiefung |
| fire poker | Schüreisen |
| ⚡ to fit the bill | das Richtige sein |

"What have you got for me then, Dr Conall?"

"John Murray, 42 years old. Died between 8 p.m. and midnight on Sunday the twenty-seventh of January. Cause was a blow to the rear of the head. Judging by the length and depth of the **indentation** to his skull, the weapon was most likely a long, heavy rod or pipe."

"Or a **fire poker**, perhaps?" Hudson asked, thinking back to the muddy footprints by the mayor's fireplace.

"That would certainly **fit the bill**."

"And how about the tartan? Does that give us any clues as to the murderer?"

"We found a few blonde hairs, about 30 centimetres in length, but the blood was all John's." Dr Conall began covering up the body.

"Good," Hudson breathed a sigh of relief. "I wanted to ask you about the other case as well, Willy MacNorris."

**Exercise 36: Unscramble the dialogue.** Lesen Sie weiter, indem Sie die folgenden Sätze in die richtige Reihenfolge bringen!

**a)** "Never mind. How about those bagpipes we found in the skip along with John Murray?"

**b)** "Actually, I was just about to come to that. You see, there were a few dog hairs on John's clothing which match those found on Willy's kilt. A white dog, by the looks of it – short-haired."

**c)** Dr Conall pulled another body out from the unit. "As anticipated, the bagpipes belong to Mr MacNorris here," she said, unzipping the second body bag.

**d)** "Hamish," Hudson muttered, **cupping his hand around** his chin.
"Sorry?"

| 1 | 2 | 3 | 4 |
|---|---|---|---|
|   |   |   |   |

"Oh goodness. He doesn't look too **chirpy**, does he, Dr Conall?"
"Nor would you, in his situation, Inspector. Anyway, take a look at this."
She pointed to a small length of wooden piping in Willy's tangled

| to cup one's hand around sth. | die Hand schützend um etw. legen |
|---|---|
| chirpy | munter |

red hair. Then she reached out to the shelves behind her for the battered bagpipes.

"They look rather the **worse for wear** now, but they would have been worth a small fortune before the accident. This is high quality **craftsmanship**; **ebony drones** and solid silver fittings."

| | |
|---|---|
| worse for wear | schäbig |
| craftsmanship | Handwerkskunst |
| ebony | Ebenholz |
| drone | *hier*: Basspfeife |
| blow pipe | Blasrohr |
| premeditated | vorsätzlich |
| intentional | mit Absicht |

"So you think Willy was carrying these when he was hit?" Hudson asked.

"Absolutely, Inspector. You see this pipe here," she pointed to its broken tip. "It snapped off on impact with the car and got caught in his mass of red curls."

"The **blow pipe** is missing entirely, though that doesn't surprise me. On a model like this, it would probably have been made of solid silver – not something the murderer would necessarily have wanted to throw away."

"Murderer? So you're certain Willy's death wasn't an accident?"

"Positive. Perhaps not **premeditated**, but certainly **intentional**. When a car accidentally hits a person crossing the road, the bruising is generally found along the side of the body. In Mr Mac-Norris' case, however, the point of impact was clearly his back, which leads me to assume that he was running away from the vehicle when it hit him. This isn't the result of a careless drunk-driver, Inspector Hudson, he or she knew exactly what they were doing."

"But why would they have taken the bagpipes and left the body?" Hudson asked.

"Perhaps because of their value… Or perhaps because the body provides us with no clues as to the make of car. The bagpipes, however, probably scratched the bonnet. The paint traces aren't

large enough to see with the naked eye but, if we're lucky, the test results will be able to tell us the colour of the car."
"Excellent." Hudson smiled for the first time that morning.

---

**Exercise 37: Adjectives and adverbs.** Formulieren Sie die Sätze neu, indem Sie die markierten Adjektive in Adverbien umwandeln oder umgekehrt!

1. Willy's **accidental** death.

   _____

2. Hudson was in **deep** thought.

   _____

3. The inspector gave the body an **uneasy** glance.

   _____

4. **Happy**, Hudson left the mortuary.

   _____

---

Meanwhile, back in Glengowan, Mrs Cartwright, the mayor's wife, was seething. Fergus had acquired the requested search warrant and the mayor's house was teeming with police officers. A team of forensic specialists was brushing for fingerprints and searching high and low for any incriminating evidence.

"And what, may I ask, is supposed to have occurred here, Sergeant Murdoch?" she hissed through clenched teeth.

"Like I said, Mrs Cartwright,

| | |
|---|---|
| seething | kochend vor Wut |
| to teem with sth. | überfüllt mit etw. |
| high and low | überall |
| incriminating evidence | belastendes Material |
| clenched teeth | zusammengebissene Zähne |

we'll just be carrying out a quick search of the office and asking a few questions. If you'd like to make yourself comfortable in the entrance hall, one of our of-

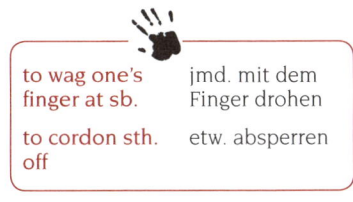

| to wag one's finger at sb. | jmd. mit dem Finger drohen |
| to cordon sth. off | etw. absperren |

ficers will be with you shortly to take your statement. We need to speak to everyone who had access to the premises last Sunday." "Make myself comfortable? This is my house, Murdoch," she said, wagging her finger at the sergeant. "Just you wait until my husband gets home…"

**Exercise 38: Translation.** Lesen Sie weiter und fügen Sie die Übersetzung der angegebenen Begriffe richtig ein!

aufklären   durchwühlen   Kofferraumklappe

Auffahrt   stoßen   Marke

Hudson arrived at the mayor's house just as the 1. _____ was being cordoned off. He flashed his 2. _____ at one of the uniformed officers and marched towards Fergus, who was 3. _____ around for some police tape in the back of his patrol car. "Right then, Sergeant. I think you've got some 4. _____ to do."
Fergus 5. _____ his head on the open 6. _____ as he stood up.

| curtly | kurz angebunden |
| sheepishly | kleinlaut |
| wits *pl* | Verstand |
| bob | *hier*: Pagenkopf |

"Inspector, you're back! How did it go with Dr…"

"No time for chitchat," Hudson said **curtly**, and flipped open his notebook.

"I'm afraid I'm going to have to pay your wife a visit," he told the sergeant. "If you could give me her address, I'll leave you in charge here a little longer."

"Hmm… That won't be necessary, Inspector," Fergus replied **sheepishly**.

"Of course it's necessary; she's officially a suspect. Though, with any luck…"

Hudson suddenly stopped talking and followed Sergeant Murdoch's gaze to where a petite figure was standing, shivering by the front door.

"That's her, I take it?" Hudson asked with a frown.

Fergus nodded.

"Have you completely lost your **wits**? What did you bring her here for?"

Before Fergus could answer, the inspector had walked over to the anxious woman.

"Mrs Murdoch?"

"Yes, Jessie," she replied nervously.

"Follow me," Hudson ordered, eyeing up her light-blonde **bob**. "We'd better get you inside, you'll catch your death."

"Th-thank you," she stuttered, rubbing her cold hands on her dress.

"Right then, Mrs Murdoch," Hudson began once they had settled down in the staff kitchen. "According to our records, your car was scrapped on Saturday afternoon in Inverness. Could you please explain why?"

Hudson poised his pencil while he waited for her to answer.

"I know what it looks like, Inspector, but… It was my son, Tommy. He's just passed his driving test. He and his mates took the car out on Friday night without me knowing; we were all at the Burns Supper, you see. It started to snow and the car skidded on some ice and crashed into a tree. It was a total wreck; I'm just thankful that the boys weren't hurt."

| to stifle | etw. unterdrücken |
| composure | Haltung |

"I take it the police were called at the time?"

"Well, no… It happened down near Munlochy. Tommy was worried that his Dad would turn up with the police so he came straight home. In a small place like this, you can understand why. He hadn't been drinking or anything… It was just unlucky, I suppose."

Jessie began to cry and Hudson pulled a tissue from his pocket.

"It's alright, Mrs Murdoch, no need to worry just yet. I'll need to talk to your son at some point, but perhaps you should go back home for now."

"I would, Inspector," Jessie sobbed, "but the police officer said all employees of the mayor's office had to wait to make a statement."

"Employee?"

Hudson **stifled** a cough and tried to keep his **composure**.

"Is there anything else that idiot husband of yours[i] hasn't told me?"

Die übliche Wendung wäre hier „your husband". Hudson sagt stattdessen „that husband of yours" und drückt damit aus, dass er augenblicklich nicht viel von Sergeant Murdoch hält.

Jessie's eyes filled with tears again.

"Sorry," Hudson added quickly. "Let's get this over and done with, then. The quicker the better."

He balanced himself on a stool in the corner of the kitchen before continuing.

**Exercise 39: Multiple choice.** Welcher Satz ist korrekt? Kreuzen Sie an!

1. a) ☐ The employees must all wait to make a statement.
   b) ☐ The employees must all wait with making their statements.

2. a) ☐ Jessie is an official declared suspect.
   b) ☐ Jessie has been officially declared a suspect.

3. a) ☐ As Jessie cries, Hudson pulled out a tissue.
   b) ☐ Hudson pulled out a tissue as Jessie began to cry.

4. a) ☐ More sooner over, more better.
   b) ☐ The sooner this is over, the better.

"So what's the nature of your employment here?"
"Cleaning lady, sir," she sobbed quietly.
"Then I suppose you have keys to the house?"
"Yes, but I've got nothing to do with whatever it is you think's gone on here…"
"Perhaps I should be the one to decide that, Mrs Murdoch. Where were you on the evening of the twenty-seventh?"
"I was at home. Tommy was still a bit shaken after the accident and we had a quiet evening in with a take-away."
"And what time did you arrive at work on Monday morning?"
"Seven-thirty."
"Was anybody else here when you arrived?"

"Daisy doesn't get here until eight-thirty, but I heard Mrs Cartwright moving about upstairs."

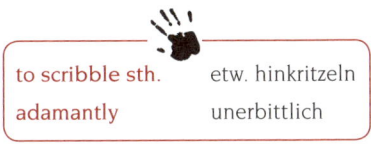

| to scribble sth. | etw. hinkritzeln |
| adamantly | unerbittlich |

Hudson nodded and **scribbled** something in his notebook.

"Did you notice anything suspicious in the mayor's office? Anything out of place?"

"No, sir," Jessie shook her head **adamantly**. "The mayor's away on business this week. Daisy said his office wouldn't need cleaning until Wednesday."

"How convenient," Hudson muttered under his breath and looked up at the officer walking towards them.

"That'll be all for now, Mrs Murdoch. Thank you for your help."

The police officer drew closer and held his hand out to the inspector.

"Constable Stanley Stawker, sir. Sergeant Murdoch put me in charge of taking down the statements, he said you'd approve."

"Very good. Go on, Constable."

"Apparently, the only other people who have access to the house are the mayor, his wife and Daisy the secretary."

Hudson poured a glass of water and signalled for him to continue.

"The mayor has been away on a business trip since Sunday morning, but no one seems to be able to get hold of him. Mrs Cartwright has an alibi; she was visiting her mother on Sunday evening. And Daisy was having dinner at Mrs Leary's house."

"Mavis?"

"Yes, Mrs Leary is Daisy's aunt."

"Well, that's a start. Thank you, Constable," Hudson declared as he walked back into the foyer.

He found Fergus a few moments later, observing the forensic team from a distance.

| meekly | kleinlaut |
|---|---|

"Very professional, Sergeant," Hudson remarked. "Good of you not to get involved, though I do wish you'd told me about your wife sooner."
"Sorry, Inspector," Fergus replied **meekly**. "I didn't know about the car until last night."
Still a little irritated, Hudson ignored the apology.
"Make sure they check the fire poker for blood and fingerprints. I've got a couple of alibis I need to follow up."
"What shall I…"
But Hudson had disappeared before Fergus could ask any more questions.

**Exercise 40: Hidden words.** In diesem Gitternetz sind sieben Polizeibegriffe versteckt. Welche sind es?

| S | I | L | W | E | M | U | R | D | E | R |
|---|---|---|---|---|---|---|---|---|---|---|
| E | T | R | A | Q | D | N | F | A | I | E |
| R | A | X | R | F | I | H | O | N | X | V |
| G | R | U | R | O | F | B | R | Q | P | I |
| E | S | T | A | T | E | M | E | N | T | D |
| A | E | G | N | T | A | A | N | I | O | E |
| N | L | K | T | E | L | I | S | S | M | N |
| T | P | V | O | W | A | J | I | L | D | C |
| O | C | R | I | M | E | S | C | E | N | E |

# 6. Every Dog Has Its Day

Mavis Leary was sipping a cup of tea behind the window of her post office, watching the comings and goings at the mayor's house with intrigue. So engrossed was she, that she did not notice Hudson entering the shop.

"Mavis?" he whispered, so as not to startle her.

"Goodness!"

Mavis turned around, spilling tea down her floral pinafore.

"I didn't mean to alarm you, Mrs Leary," Hudson said apologetically.

"It's quite alright, Inspector," she smiled, a little flustered. "Serves me right for being a nosy old busybody."

"I was wondering if you could tell me what you were doing on Sunday the twenty-seventh between 7 p.m. and midnight."

"Yes, of course. Let me think…"

Mavis stood for a moment, dabbing her apron.

| pinafore | Schürze |
| busybody | Topfgucker |
| to dab | tupfen |

"Ah, of course! Daisy came over for dinner. She was upset about her latest heartbreak and spent the entire evening sobbing over my roast chicken."

"May I be so indiscreet as to ask who this gentleman might be?"

"I'm not one to gossip, Inspector, but seeing as this is an investigation… His name's Gregor."

"Do carry on," Hudson prompted.

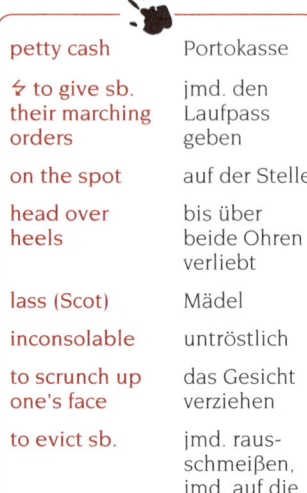

| | |
|---|---|
| petty cash | Portokasse |
| ⚡ to give sb. their marching orders | jmd. den Laufpass geben |
| on the spot | auf der Stelle |
| head over heels | bis über beide Ohren verliebt |
| lass (Scot) | Mädel |
| inconsolable | untröstlich |
| to scrunch up one's face | das Gesicht verziehen |
| to evict sb. | jmd. rausschmeißen, jmd. auf die Straße setzen |

"He's the Cartwrights' gardener or, better said, was. You must have heard about him while you were at the mayor's house."

Hudson took a deep breath. "No, Mrs Leary, unfortunately not. Would you mind telling me some more about this Mr…"

"Williams. Gregor Williams. He's a nice enough lad, I suppose. Can't be much over thirty. He worked in the gardens for the last year or so but, just before Christmas, they caught him stealing from the **petty cash**. Gregor was **given his marching orders on the spot**."

"I see," Hudson remarked. "And he and Miss Malden were a couple?"

"No, no, Inspector. Daisy was **head over heels** for him, and for a while it seemed as though the feeling was mutual. But then he suddenly started to give her the cold shoulder, and the poor **lass** has been **inconsolable** ever since he left."

"Do you know where I might be able to find Mr Williams?" Hudson asked.

Mavis paused and **scrunched up her** wrinkled little **face**.

"Afraid not, Inspector," she replied. "I think he lived down in South Gowan, but I've heard rumours of him having been **evicted**. He has a sister, Sophie. Perhaps he's staying with her."

"Wonderful. At least I can rely on you, Mavis."

"Oh, Inspector, you're too kind," she said, flattered. "Here, take something to keep your strength up," she insisted, putting a packet of shortbread into his coat pocket.

**Exercise 41: Odd one out.** Welches Wort ist das „schwarze Schaf"? Unterstreichen Sie!

1. sip   slurp   swallow   saliva
2. apologize   regret   remorse   be sorry
3. gossip   rumour   report   hearsay
4. mutual   mismatched   joint   common

Hudson shut the post office door firmly behind him. He was standing in the shelter of the doorway, wrapping himself up against the icy wind, when Fergus' car pulled up in front.

"Going anywhere nice, Inspector?" Fergus called out through the half-opened window. "I can give you a lift if you like."

Hudson looked up at the ominously heavy clouds.

"Alright then, Sergeant. Take me to Nessie Nostalgia."

"But only if you tell me what Dr Conall had to say," Fergus insisted as Hudson climbed into the passenger seat.

| to drive a hard bargain | hart verhandeln |
| intently | konzentriert |
| to swerve | kurven |

"You **drive a hard bargain**, Sergeant!" Hudson said with a laugh, and proceeded to recount the morning's events.

Fergus listened **intently**, clutching the small steering wheel as the car **swerved** along the country roads.

"Maybe whoever it was killed Willy for his bagpipes. You know, perhaps they needed the money… And maybe John witnessed the hit-and-run and they had to kill him, too!" Fergus proudly announced his theory.

**Exercise 42: Fill in the blanks.** Lesen Sie weiter und vervollständigen Sie den Text!

"Nice **1.** i_____, Sergeant, but I fear things are a little more **2.** c_____ than that. I spoke to John on the **3.** a_____ before he died and he **4.** m_____ nothing about Willy, barely knew anything about the man. There must be another **5.** c_____, perhaps one neither of them were even **6.** a_____ existed. I think we need to find out what Willy was doing between the time Father Angus saw him leave the village hall at 11 p.m. and his death just after midnight. Perhaps it has something to do with the woman Duncan **7.** h_____ sobbing in the cloakroom."

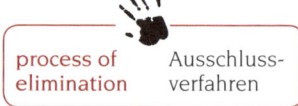

| process of elimination | Ausschlussverfahren |

"Whoever it was, Inspector, they would have needed their car to transport John's body from the house to the dump, so they can't have had it scrapped after hitting Willy…"

"I know what you're trying to say, Fergus," Hudson replied calmly. "By process of elimination, it can't have been your wife. But she's still a suspect nonetheless. Blonde hairs were found on the tartan covering John's body; you have to admit, it does look suspicious."

"I know, I know," Fergus said apologetically. "Though I wonder what John was doing at the mayor's house in the first place."

"That's what I'm hoping to find out, Sergeant," Hudson said as

| | |
|---|---|
| to falter | zaudern |
| dusk | Abenddämmerung |
| to clamber out of sth. | aus etw. klettern |
| woefully | elend |
| jest | Spaß |

the car pulled up beneath the orange awning of the souvenir shop.

"In the meantime, I need you to check out Mrs Cartwright's alibi and find out the whereabouts of Gregor Williams for me: someone else you failed to tell me about."

Fergus stiffened.

"Look, Inspector," he **faltered**, not knowing how to explain. "He doesn't work there any more, I thought…"

"Save it for later; I need to get going before **dusk** falls," Hudson said, **clambering out of** the police car. "What interests me more is the whereabouts of that damn mayor. How can Mrs Cartwright not know where her own husband is?"

"Apparently he's been keeping a few secrets from her recently. She seemed awfully upset. I reckon he's cheating on her if you ask me."

"Another happy couple in Glengowan," Hudson said sarcastically.

Fergus looked **woefully** at the dashboard.

| Wendungen mit pull | |
|---|---|
| to pull up | stoppen (Fahrzeug) |
| to pull out | ausscheren, abfahren |
| to pull through | durchkommen |
| to pull the strings | die Strippen ziehen |
| to pull rank | den Vorgesetzten rauskehren |

"Sorry, Fergus," Hudson sighed. "It was only meant in **jest**. Just get hold of him by tonight, otherwise I'm going to have to send out a search squad."

**Exercise 43: True or false?** Welche Aussagen sind korrekt? Markieren Sie mit richtig ✔ oder falsch – !

1. John's body was transported by car. ☐

2. Despite the blonde hairs, Jessie is no longer a main suspect. ☐

3. Hudson is dismayed by Fergus' lack of cooperation. ☐

4. Sergeant Murdoch presumes the mayor's marriage is on the rocks. ☐

---

Hudson gave the roof of the car a friendly pat and sent the sergeant on his way. He walked towards the shop; the sea of Loch Ness Monster figurines appeared curiously forbidding in the semi-darkness of the unlit window. Hudson's eye caught the handwritten "Back in 10" sign hanging from the handle of the locked door. He jiggled it a few times, but to no avail.
I thought you might have, Hudson thought to himself as he turned towards the small pathway that John had pointed out to him on Sunday. Suddenly the skies opened with an almighty crack of thunder and Hudson began to walk quickly.

Ten minutes later, he emerged, cold and wet, on the shore of Loch Ness. Lightning flashed through the valley and a small dog came running in leaps and bounds through the pouring rain.
"Here boy!" Hudson called out,

| | |
|---|---|
| forbidding | bedrohlich |
| to jiggle | rütteln |
| to no avail | vergebens |
| in leaps and bounds | in großen Sprüngen |

bending down to greet the terrier. "You must be Hamish. Want to show me where you live?"

| puffing and panting | schnaufend und keuchend |
| crumpled | zerknautscht |

The little white ball of fur dashed off along the muddy beach in the direction of Willy's hut. Hudson arrived, **puffing and panting**, a few moments later. The front door stood wide open and he entered tentatively, unsure as to what he might find. But whatever the inspector had expected, it certainly wasn't this. Inch upon inch, wall upon wall, the entire hut was one disorderly homage to the Loch Ness Monster. Hudson shuffled through the mass of scattered newspapers; barely able to see the floor, he stepped into a **crumpled** packet of Nessie Nosh dog food.

Disgusting, he thought, wiping his shoe on a copy of Nessie Weekly.

**Exercise 44: Unscramble. Lesen Sie weiter und ordnen Sie die Buchstaben zu sinnvollen Wörtern!**

It wasn't long before the inspector's **1. cteppeiver** _____ eyes had discovered the **2. sboiunrlac** _____ and yellowing diary by the window. He picked up the latter and **3. ludpmpe** _____ himself down on the small bed. The dusty mattress **4. kerdace** _____ loudly under his weight, startling the **5. souixna** _____ inspector. Leafing through the pages, he found endless accounts of Nessie **6. stghigisn** _____.

| | |
|---|---|
| hump | Buckel |
| ⚡ loopy | durchgeknallt |
| concede | einräumen, zugeben |
| to make a nuisance of oneself | andere belästigen |
| to scramble | *hier:* klettern |
| legible | lesbar |
| to decipher | entziffern |

"July the fourth," he read aloud, "9:18 p.m. Waters rough, possible sighting of **hump** to the south-east… August the eigth: calm evening, no sign of N. August the ninth: brief glimpse of…"

The entries were, on the whole, of no interest to Hudson. As far as he was concerned, the bagpiper had clearly been a little **loopy**. What did interest the inspector, however, were the pages he couldn't see. Almost two months of entries following the twenty-ninth of November were missing.

He pulled himself up off the bed and made to leave the hut. Hamish sat in the doorway, wagging his tail expectantly.

"Oh, alright," Hudson **conceded**. "But don't **make a nuisance of yourself**."

Dripping wet, Hudson and his new-found friend entered the Loch Inn through the back door so as not to attract Dorothy's attention. They **scrambled** up the staircase and into the warmth of his bedroom. Hudson quickly changed into some dry clothes and lay Hamish down in front of the fire with a blanket.

He took out Willy's diary and the burnt pages from the mayor's fireplace and sat down at the small writing desk. The charred pages were barely **legible**, but Hudson could see that the handwriting matched. The few words that he could make out, however, had nothing to do with the Loch Ness Monster.

"December the…," Hudson struggled to read the fragmented sentences. "MC arrives, 6 p.m. …Gregor at the east shore…"

He paused for a moment at the name Gregor before trying to **decipher** more.

"Inspector!"
Dorothy's piercing scream echoed through the house. Hudson ran out to the landing and looked down from the top of the staircase to the hallway below. Mrs Murdoch stood staring red-faced back up at him, holding a mop and bucket.

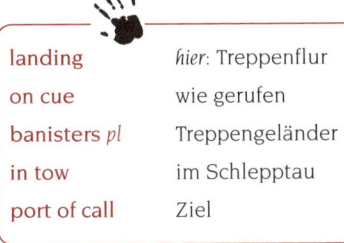

| landing | *hier*: Treppenflur |
| on cue | wie gerufen |
| banisters *pl* | Treppengeländer |
| in tow | im Schlepptau |
| port of call | Ziel |

"Have you seen the state of my carpet? There are muddy footprints leading all through the kitchen and up the stairs right to your door! And by the looks of it, you've brought something four-legged back home with you as well."

Just on cue, Hamish trotted out of Hudson's room and poked his inquisitive little head through the banisters.

"So sorry, Mrs Murdoch… Afraid I've got to dash, just leave me the bill for the carpet cleaning…"

Before she could answer, Hudson had slipped down the stairs and out of the front door, the small Scottie dog obediently in tow. The pair walked quickly to the police station, where Hudson hoped to find Fergus. He was in luck, and they all climbed into the police car and sped off to their next port of call.

**Exercise 45: Word forms.** Ergänzen Sie das jeweilige Substantiv und Adverb!

1. interesting _____ _____
2. intended _____ _____
3. angered _____ _____
4. obedient _____ _____

| derelict | verfallen |

"Would you mind telling your friend to stop gnawing at my seat belts, Inspector?" Fergus asked irritably, eyeing up the excited terrier through his rear-view mirror.

Hudson distracted Hamish with some shortbread from his pocket and continued their conversation.

"So, tell me about Mrs Cartwright. Was she really with her mother on Sunday night?"

"It's hard to say, exactly."

"Well either she was, or she wasn't."

"You see, sir, Mrs Farrow appears to suffer from Alzheimer's. It was difficult enough trying to get her to remember she had a daughter at all, let alone whether Caitlin visited her on Sunday or not."

"I see," Hudson said sympathetically. "Does she lives alone?"

"Yes, unless you count the dozen cats jumping around the place," Fergus replied wish a shudder. "It's like a zoo in there. And the neighbours didn't see anything either. Perhaps we'll just have to take Caitlin's word for it."

"Hmm…," Hudson replied quietly. "Or perhaps she's just lying."

"Always the suspicious one, Inspector!" Fergus chuckled.

"All part of the job, Fergus."

**Exercise 46: Verb forms.** Lesen Sie weiter und ergänzen Sie die fehlenden Verbformen!

| ring | wait | stop | peer | look | go |

It wasn't long before they **1.** _____ outside a **derelict** house a few miles down the road in South Gowan.

"Here we 2.           , Inspector," Fergus said. "This is where Gregor Williams lives."

Constable Stawker 3.           in the porch. Hudson 4.           the doorbell and 5.           impatiently through the letterbox.

" 6.           like no one's in; perhaps we should leave," Fergus suggested.

---

"Don't give up so easily, Fergus," Hudson scolded him. "Give me a leg up, Stanley," he said, pointing to a window that was slightly ajar.

"Perhaps we should wait for the search warrant, Inspector," the constable suggested.

"Can't afford to, Constable.

| to scold sb. | jmd. schimpfen |
|---|---|
| ajar | angelehnt |

There's something suspicious about this Gregor fellow. His name is mentioned in Willy's diary. I'm fairly certain that he has something to do with the murders."

Hudson landed on the living room floor with a thud.

"What exactly are we looking for, Inspector?" Fergus asked after Hudson had let the two officers in through the front door.

The inspector held out his hand and revealed a shiny silver whistle.

"This will do nicely," he smiled.

"What's that?" Stanley asked, taking a closer look.

"It's the missing blow pipe from Willy's bagpipes. Solid silver, just as Dr Conall predicted."

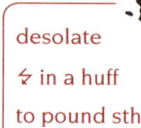

| | |
|---|---|
| desolate | trostlos |
| ⚡ in a huff | verärgert |
| to pound sth. | auf/an etw. hämmern |

"He certainly could do with the money. This place is falling apart," Stanley said, giving the shabby, **desolate** rooms a cursory glance.

"What do you mean, Stawker?"

"Best let Fergus explain. He knows Gregor a bit better, don't you old fellow?" Stanley said laughing.

"Is there something else you're not telling me, Sergeant Murdoch?" Hudson demanded, his smile rapidly disappearing.

"I did try to tell you before, sir…," the sergeant answered hesitantly. "Gregor is sort of the reason why Jessie and I are getting divorced…"

"Excellent!" Hudson exclaimed, walking off to the car **in a huff**. "Two of our main suspects are having an affair and no one bothered to mention it to me. How cosy!"

Fergus and Stanley both followed Hudson apprehensively to the car.

"Stanley, come with me. We're going to find Gregor and take him down for questioning. As for you, Fergus, I'm taking you off the case before I have to arrest you as well."

Fergus stared shamefacedly at the pavement.

"You'll find him at his sister's place, 43 Thistle Road. Her name is Sophie Jewell. He was evicted from here last week for not paying the rent."

"Better late than never," Hudson snapped, slamming the car door behind him.

Hudson sped off, Stanley clutching Hamish in the back seat, while Fergus was left standing alone on the wet pavement.

Sophie Jewell was just putting her daughter to bed when there was a loud **pounding** at the door.

"Police! Open up!"

Hudson had brought his bad mood with him.

"We'd like to speak to your brother please, Ms Jewell," he demanded.

---

**Exercise 47: Unscramble the sentences.** Bringen Sie die Wörter in die richtige Reihenfolge!

1. presence  Hudson  diary  the  the  Gregor's  suspicious  finds  name  of  in

   _____
   _____

2. through  window  Hudson  letting  climbed  the  before  in  officers  the  in

   _____
   _____

3. that  having  inspector  were  two  told  his  was  suspects  not  affair  the  an  of  main

   _____
   _____

4. off  as  case  well  taken  Fergus  before  is  he  the  arrested  is

   _____
   _____

Sophie stared wide-eyed[i] at the two policemen.

"I-I-I... What do you want?" she asked, starting to shake.

"We've reason to believe that your brother Gregor is connected to the recent murders in Glengowan. Where is he?" Hudson asked her.

"He's just popped out to get some milk; he should be back in a minute. I-I-I knew Gregor was in a bit of trouble, but I never would have thought..."

"What kind of trouble, Ms Jewell?"

"Well, you know, with the gambling and everything. He owed a lot of people money. I said he could stay here until he got back on his feet. He's so good with little Polly," she said, swaying the toddler in her arms.

"Who exactly did he owe money to?" Hudson asked.

"Well, everybody... Jessie Murdoch leant him a fair bit, she's been so kind. But I think he owed a Mr Murray a few thousand as well."

"John Murray?"

"Yes, I think so."

Suddenly the latch on the front door clicked.

"Don't worry, only me!" Gregor shouted cheerily as he walked into the small sitting room.

Their eyes briefly met, and Hudson watched as the shiny white milk bottle slipped from Gregor's hands and landed with a crash on the wooden floor.

---

**Compound adjectives**

Adjektive, die aus zwei oder mehr Begriffen bestehen, werden oft mit Bindestrich verbunden. Nur selten werden sie zusammengeschrieben (z.B. lovesick).

Im britischen Englisch werden die Einzelbegriffe v.a. dann mit einem Bindestrich verbunden, wenn ein zusammengesetztes Adjektiv als Attribut vor einem Substantiv steht.

Hinter dem Substantiv stehen die Begriffe auch oft einzeln:

The much-loved parish priest.
The priest was much loved.

**Exercise 48: Word spiral.** Finden Sie die Begriffe in der Wortspirale!

| 1 | 2 | 3 | 4 | 5 | 6 | 7 | 8 |
|---|---|---|---|---|---|---|---|
| 24 | 25 | 26 | 27 | 28 | 29 | 30 | 9 |
| 23 | 40 | 41 | 42 | 43 | 44 | 31 | 10 |
| 22 | 39 | 48 | 47 | 46 | 45 | 32 | 11 |
| 21 | 38 | 37 | 36 | 35 | 34 | 33 | 12 |
| 20 | 19 | 18 | 17 | 16 | 15 | 14 | 13 |

- **1-10.** ready to reveal secrets
- **10-15.** a hypothesis
- **15-17.** sound a dog makes
- **17-22.** knocks on the door
- **22-32.** of a person who is kind and sensitive
- **32-43.** to give someone this is to be very unfriendly (2 words)
- **43-48.** a circulating story of doubtful truth

# 7. The Truth Will Out

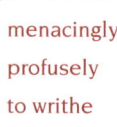

| | |
|---|---|
| menacingly | bedrohlich |
| profusely | reichlich |
| to writhe | sich drehen und winden |

It was late and heavy black clouds hung **menacingly** low over the sleeping village of Glengowan as Hudson and Constable Stawker escorted Gregor Williams back to the police station. Hudson could hear Gregor cursing **profusely** under his breath as they walked up the gravel driveway to the small station. He wriggled and **writhed** in Stanley's firm grip until they threatened him with handcuffs and a night in the cells.

**Exercise 49: Fill in the blanks.** Lesen Sie weiter und setzen Sie die Ausdrücke in der korrekten Form ein!

reply vehement    freeze    clear one's throat    have
shiver    bellow    switch on

"So, Mr Williams," Hudson's voice **1.** _____ through the empty station as they sat down at a bare wooden desk. "I think it's time we **2.** _____ a proper chat, don't you?"

"I've got nothing to say to you, Hudson," Gregor **3.** ▓▓▓▓▓▓▓▓. "I've done nothing wrong!"

Hudson noticed him **4.** ▓▓▓▓▓▓▓▓ in his chair and went to turn up the heating.

"Bring us a **brew**, would you Stanley?" Hudson called out to the kitchen. "It's **5.** ▓▓▓▓▓▓▓▓ in here!"

Hudson sat back down and **6.** ▓▓▓▓▓▓▓▓ before **7.** ▓▓▓▓▓▓▓▓ the cassette recorder on the table between them.

---

"Right then. If you've done nothing wrong, why don't you tell me how this fine **specimen** came to be in your possession?"

Gregor took one look at the silver blowpipe in the inspector's hands and leant himself back in his chair with a demonstrative groan.

"Alright," Hudson sighed, taking another approach. "I hear you owed John Murray some money. Why don't you tell me some more about that?"

| | |
|---|---|
| **brew** | Tee |
| **specimen** | Exemplar |
| **to retort** | antworten |

"I just placed a few unlucky bets, that's all. John lent me some money after the mayor kicked me out; you know, to pay the rent and that. I thought I'd place it on a horse first and double my luck, but it fell on the fifth hurdle and I lost everything. So I had to borrow some more and, well…"

"Would you say you had a gambling addiction, Mr Williams?"

"Would you say that it was none of your business, Mr Hudson?" Gregor **retorted**.

| ⚡ to be rolling in it | sehr reich sein |
| --- | --- |
| ⚡ whopping | riesig |
| miser | Geizhals |

"Alright, no need for that attitude. Do you still have keys to the Cartwright residence?"

"Might have. If you let me go, I'll have a look at home."

"I don't think so. What would you say if I suggested it would have been easier for you to get rid of John Murray altogether rather than repay the few thousand pounds you owed him?"

"I'd say that I was babysitting Polly the night he was killed, so it can't have been me. I'm no criminal, Inspector."

"Apart from the incident with the petty cash."

"Oh come on, it was just a few bob. That mayor's rolling in it. He's just bought himself a whopping great manor house in England and the old miser can't afford to lend me twenty quid to buy my niece a Christmas present."

"Is that so?" Hudson asked, intrigued.

---

**Exercise 50: What would have happened?** Vervollständigen Sie die if-Sätze!

1. If Gregor has done nothing wrong, how come

   _____

2. Gregor might not be in so much debt if

   _____

3. If Hudson lets him go, Gregor will

   _____

4. _____

   if the mayor had lent him money.

Before he could continue, Stanley entered, rattling a tray of tea and biscuits in front of him.

| unyielding | unnachgiebig |
| obstinate | dickköpfig |

"Anything else I can get you, sir?"

"No thank you, Constable. Things are just about to get interesting."

Hudson poured them both a cup of tea and made himself as comfortable as he could in the hard, unyielding chair.

"Where were you on the night of the twenty-fifth of January?" he asked, glaring at the obstinate gardener.

"I was at the Burns Supper, just like everyone else," Gregor snarled. "Ask your Dorothy, she saw me."

"And what time did you leave the village hall?"

"Just before midnight. I would have left earlier but when I went to collect my things, I found Mrs Cartwright in the back of the cloakroom. She was all in tears. I hung around for a bit to make sure she was alright, but she just told me to get lost. She's always been the ungrateful sort."

"I see," Hudson nodded, appreciative of the gardener's growing cooperation. "And did you notice anything suspicious after you left?"

"Depends on what you mean by suspicious."

"You know very well what I mean. A dead body, that sort of thing."

"Aye, as it happens, I did."

Hudson raised his eyebrows, he hadn't expected an answer like that.

"Yeh, I was walking down the road back to Sophie's and I heard a car screeching. When I turned around, Willy was running away but the car got the better of him."

"And that's when you found the pipe?"

"Well done, Sherlock."

| | |
|---|---|
| to wince | zucken |
| to tamper with sth. | unerlaubte Änderungen an etw. vornehmen |
| to intervene | dazwischenfahren |
| na | nein |

Hudson **winced** at the comparison.

"Obviously I went over to see if I could help, but he was clearly dead. The pipe had broken off his bagpipes and was lying in the gutter next to him. I didn't think he'd mind."

"You knew Mr MacNorris, did you?"

"Not really, just by sight, but…"

"**Tampering** with evidence is a serious crime," Hudson **intervened**. "As is failing to report a murder."

"Come off it, Inspector. I'm in enough trouble as it is, I didn't want to get involved in a murder investigation as well."

"Looks like it's too late for that. Did you see the driver, or notice what make the car was?"

---

**Exercise 51: Translation.** Lesen Sie weiter und fügen Sie die Übersetzung der angegebenen Begriffe richtig ein!

flüsterte etwas | Handlungsweise | es passierte alles

seine Entscheidung | ich erinnere mich | können

es scheint

"**Na**, it was dark and 1. _____ so quickly… I think the car was silver, though, 2. _____ it shining in the moonlight."

Before Hudson could continue, Constable Stawker walked up behind the inspector and  3.           into his ear.

"About time, too!" Hudson exclaimed, leaping up from his chair. "Alright, Gregor, let's call it a night.  4.           I've got no grounds to keep you in on, so you  5.           go home. I'll be keeping an eye on you, mind, so no **shifty** business."

Gregor took flight before Hudson could **repeal**  6.          , and the two policemen sat in the **draughty** station planning their next  7.           until the early hours of the morning.

The birds were already beginning their morning chorus when Hudson crept into the Loch Inn a few hours later. He stole into the warm kitchen to make himself a strong cup of coffee before setting off on his next mission and was startled to see a small figure **crouched** in front of the fireplace.

"Dorothy? You frightened the life out of me!"

"Sorry, Mr Hudson, I can't sleep. Fergus ran off this evening in a terrible **flap** about being taken off the case and hasn't come home yet. God help him, the poor **laddie**."

| | |
|---|---|
| **shifty** | unaufrichtig |
| **to repeal sth.** | etw. widerrufen |
| **draughty** | zugig |
| **to crouch** | (sich) zusammenkauern |
| **⚡ in a flap** | aufgeregt |
| **laddie (Scot)** | Bursche |

"I'm sorry, Mrs Murdoch," Hudson replied softly. "Really, I had no choice."

"I understand. It's just… He's a sensitive boy at heart. He didn't mean to do any wrong."

Hudson placed his arm around her delicate shoulders.

"I'm sure he'll turn up soon, perhaps you'd best get off to bed."

"Yes, perhaps you're right."

"Just one question…," Hudson added before she reached the door.

"Yes?" she asked, turning around in her flannel nightdress.

"Do the initials MC mean anything to you?"

"No, Inspector, I can't say they do."

"Never mind. Thank you, Dorothy."

"Goodnight, Inspector."

Hudson sat in the warmth of the fire and listened to the landlady's **nimble** footsteps climbing the stairs to bed.

| | |
|---|---|
| nimble | flink |
| contentedly | zufrieden |

---

**Exercise 52: Synonyms.** Lesen Sie weiter und unterstreichen Sie die Entsprechungen zu den folgenden Begriffen!

baggage   enter   unwary   comfortably

The clock struck 9 a.m. as the express train from Edinburgh pulled into Inverness station early that Wednesday morning. Quentin Cartwright had been sitting **contentedly** in his carriage, sipping tea and puzzling over the morning's crossword. He gathered his belongings and

> waited for the doors to open, ready to embrace a busy day back in the office. **Unbeknown** to him, however, Stanley Stawker and his team of police officers had lined the station platform, waiting to **pounce** on the unsuspecting mayor.

"Good morning, Mr Cartwright. If you'd like to come with me, please."

His feet had barely touched the platform when Quentin felt a firm hand grip his upper arm and lead him out towards a row of police cars waiting at the entrance.

"What on earth… Are you arresting me?"

"If you cooperate, I won't have to," Stanley replied, enjoying his new-found authority. "The inspector has a few questions he'd like to ask you down at the station regarding the murders of Willy MacNorris and John Murray."

"Murder? I didn't even know John was dead!" the mayor shouted back at the wilful officer, beginning to fear what they had in store for him as they **bundled him into** the back of a car.

Just moments later, they were driving up Longman Road to the Northern Constabulary headquarters.

"What are you bringing me here for?" Quentin asked, panicking at the sight of the formidable red building.

"Inspector Hudson thought it might be more convenient," Stanley explained, his voice echoing as they marched along the **austere** hallway.

| | |
|---|---|
| unbeknown to sb. | ohne jds. Wissen |
| to pounce on sb. | sich auf jmd. stürzen |
| to bundle sb. into sth. | jmd. verfrachten in |
| austere | karg |

| | |
|---|---|
| hardened criminal | Schwerverbrecher |
| to clack | klappern |
| flagstone | Steinplatte |

"But this is where they bring the hardened criminals."

"For all we know, sir, you might be one of them. Take a seat; the inspector will be with you shortly."

Stanley locked the door of the bleak interrogation room behind him, leaving the mayor to wait, frightened and alone.

**Exercise 53: Reported speech.** Verwandeln Sie die Sätze in die indirekte Rede!

1. "If you'd like to come with me, Mr Cartwright," asked Stanley.

   _____

2. "Are you arresting me?" the mayor asked angrily.

   _____

3. "I didn't even know John was dead!" the mayor shouted back.

   _____

4. "Inspector Hudson thought it might be more convenient," Stanley's voice echoed.

   _____

Back in the comparable idyll of Glengowan, a smartly-dressed figure walked across the quiet village square. Her shiny high heels clacked loudly across the wet flagstones, along the driveway and up the steps to the mayor's house. Reaching the doorway, she quickly reapplied her lipstick and patted her wavy red hair into place before pulling at the heavy doorbell.

| | |
|---|---|
| persuasive | konsequent |
| to yank sth. | an etw. ziehen |
| to pout | schmollen |
| to flop | hinplumpsen |

Inside, Daisy Malden was sitting behind her orderly desk, typing up some letters.

"We're closed today," she shouted, without looking up or leaving her seat.

The doorbell rang again.

"But I've got an appointment with Quentin," came the **persuasive** reply from the other side of the door.

Daisy got up with a groan and **yanked** open the front door.

"Mr Cartwright isn't available today, you'll have to come back next week," she snapped in her usual abrupt tone as she looked the red-headed woman up and down.

"You're not from around here, are you? What do you want?" she asked.

"Una Breannan. Quentin asked me to be here at 11:30 a.m. May I come in?" she insisted, pushing her way through into the hallway.

"I just told you he's not available. Please leave," Daisy demanded, still standing by the open door.

"Well where is he, then? I'll wait," Una **pouted**, **flopping** down on one of the armchairs in the foyer.

"I'm not at liberty to say, but there's no point in waiting: he won't be back today."

"Very well," Una gave in reluctantly. "Here's my card, tell him to call me the second he gets back. I'll be staying at the Loch Inn."

Daisy shut the door without saying goodbye and threw the pink business card into the bin before returning to her desk.

**Exercise 54: Translation.** Lesen Sie weiter und übersetzen Sie die folgenden Sätze ins Deutsche!

A short while later, a few miles down the road at Glengowan wool mill, Mrs MacDougal was **reclining drowsily** in her steaming bubble bath. Duncan came in and **perched** himself on the edge of the **brimming** tub.
"How's the backache, sweetheart?" he asked, rubbing her wet shoulders.
"A bit better thanks, dear," Morag said, getting up out of the bath and **swathing** herself in a large blue towel.

"Good. Well I've got to get going with the deliveries, but I'll be back before dinner. You just put your feet up and keep yourself out of trouble, you hear?"
"Yes, dear," Morag smiled at her husband, trying not to let on how much pain she

| to recline | sich zurücklegen |
| drowsily | schläfrig |
| to perch | hocken |
| brimming | bis zum Rande gefüllt |
| to swathe | einwickeln |

was in. "Don't you worry. It'll just be me, my knitting and a bit of daytime telly."

| | |
|---|---|
| **surge** | plötzlicher Anstieg |
| **contraction** | Wehe |
| **to scuttle** | hoppeln |
| **to hurtle** | rasen |

"There's a good girl," Duncan said, kissing his wife goodbye.

She listened to him rummaging around in the kitchen while she dressed.

"I can't find my mobile, love," he shouted up to the bathroom. "But I won't be gone long."

"Alright dear, I'm sure I can cope without you for an hour or two."

After a few minutes, the front door clicked shut and Morag slowly made her way down the stairs. Before she could reach the last step, however, she was overcome by a huge **surge** of pain. Grabbing hold of the banisters, she breathed her way as calmly as she could through the first **contraction**.

"Duncan!" she yelled at the top her voice, in the hope that her husband was still outside. "Duncan! Are you there?"

Hearing no answer, she walked painfully to the front door and looked out. She could see Duncan's van turning at the end of the driveway and **scuttled** as fast as she could towards it, waving her arms to attract his attention. But it was no use. By the time she reached the main road, Duncan was well out of sight and the second contraction was coming on heavily. Frightened, alone, and overwhelmed with pain, Morag knelt sobbing at the side of the road. She was just thinking about how best to get to the hospital, when a small sports car came **hurtling** towards the mill. Morag saw her chance and crawled out onto the road, forcing the car to come to a halt. Morag recognized the face of Caitlin Cartwright behind the wheel.

"Oh, thank goodness!" Morag cried in relief. "Please, help me."

Caitlin tried her best to shake off the hysterical pregnant woman.

| profanity | Obszönität |

"I'm really sorry, Morag, it's not a good time…"

"It's not a good time for me, either, you silly woman," Morag shouted back while she bundled herself into the passenger seat. "But there's not much we can do about it now, so just get me to the hospital!"

Unable to refuse, Caitlin reluctantly reignited the engine, muttering a long succession of profanities under her breath.

---

**Exercise 55: Match up the phrases.** Welche der folgenden Satzteile gehören zusammen? Ordnen Sie zu!

1. ☐ surge     a) profanities
2. ☐ at the top     b) of pain
3. ☐ mutter     c) without someone else
4. ☐ cope     d) of one's voice

---

"So, Mr Cartwright," Hudson announced loudly, flinging his bulging case file onto the desk of the interrogation room. "Nice of you to finally join us."

"If I'd have known you were looking for me, Inspector, I would have come sooner, but…"

"So where exactly have you been hiding, then?"

"I was in Edinburgh for a meeting," Quentin protested.

"For four days?"

"Well, yes… There was a lot to discuss."

"And you couldn't tell your wife about this meeting?"

"It was meant to be a surprise."

"You call cheating on your wife a surprise? I'm sure she'll be delighted," Hudson remarked provocatively.

"I'm not having an affair, Mr Hudson!"

| | |
|---|---|
| extramarital | außerehelich |
| indiscretion | Unüberlegtheit |
| to gloat | sich hämisch freuen |
| haven | Oase |

Hudson leant forwards, their faces almost touching.

"Look, Mr Cartwright; I'm not here to judge. Just tell me what's going on and I'll try to keep any **extramarital indiscretions** to myself. As far as I can tell, you were one of the last people to see both Willy MacNorris and John Murray alive. A bit of a coincidence, don't you think?"

Quentin pulled away from the inspector's menacing glare.

"Okay, here's the deal. I'm not cheating on Caitlin, but I haven't been entirely honest with her, or the other villagers, either."

"Now we're getting somewhere," Hudson **gloated**, crossing his arms against his chest.

"I was made an offer just before Christmas by a building developer in Edinburgh. The company wants to build a holiday resort in Glengowan, overlooking Loch Ness. It's a lucrative deal; I couldn't let it pass."

"Hence the secretive meetings? I don't understand why you couldn't tell your wife, though."

"I couldn't tell anyone, Mr Hudson. The villagers are so proud of their little **haven**, if word got out about the resort there'd be protests left, right and centre. I couldn't let them ruin it… We need the money."

"You mean you need the money?" Hudson proposed. "That beautiful English mansion won't pay for itself now, will it?"

"How did you…?"

"Never mind about that. How much were they offering for the land?"

"Almost ten million. More than enough to renovate the village church, finance more resources for the local school…"

"And buy yourself a house?"

| | |
|---|---|
| mortgage | Hypothek |
| to catch wind of sth. | etw. kapieren |
| dumbstruck | sprachlos |

"Yes, and that, too. I wanted it to be a surprise for Caitlin, she's been begging for us to move away from the village for years."

"Right, so you've been keeping this big secret for the last few months, terrified that if someone finds out, the villagers will file a petition and you'll be landed with a **mortgage** that you can't pay off."

"Well, if you put it like that…"

"Unfortunately for you," Hudson briskly continued, "Mr MacNorris **caught wind** of your plans and confronted you at the Burns Supper. You thought you'd solved the problem when you ran him over, until John Murray turned up at your office on Sunday night wanting to know more, so you killed him as well."

Quentin froze in his chair.

"Am I correct, Mr Cartwright? After all, who's to say you really were already in Edinburgh on Sunday night?"

The mayor opened his mouth to object[i], but nothing came out.

"Quentin Cartwright, I'm arresting you on suspicion of murder. You do not have to say anything,

**Betonung Verb vs. Nomen**
Bei Begriffen, die sowohl Verb als auch Nomen sein können, wird das Verb auf der zweiten Silbe betont, das Nomen aber immer auf der ersten Silbe:
to ob'ject   the 'object
to con'sole  the 'console
to re'cord   the 'record

but it may harm your defence if you do not mention when questioned something which you later rely on in court…"

**Dumbstruck**, the mayor listened while the inspector fastened the handcuffs around his wrists and led him towards the cells.

**Exercise 56: Crossword puzzle.** Lösen Sie das Kreuzworträtsel!

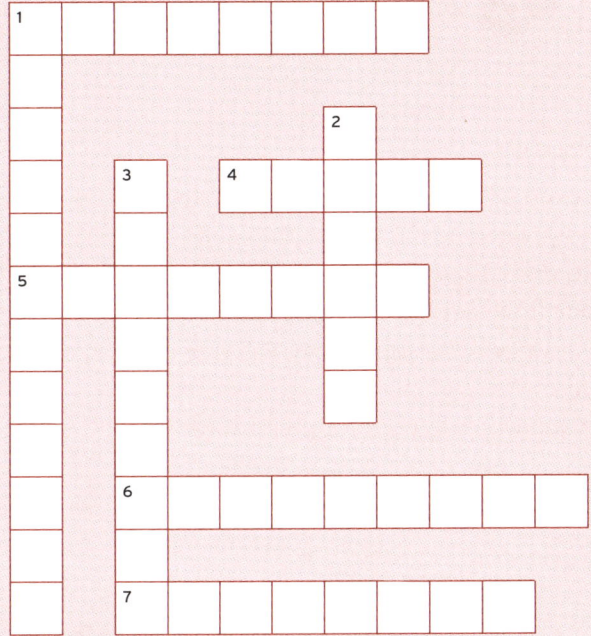

### Across
1. not the exit, but the...
4. boast or show malicious pleasure
5. synonym for threatening
6. a place to snuggle up to
7. a piece of evidence

### Down
1. occurring outside marriage
2. jump like a cat
3. used to control arrested persons

# 8 Pride Comes Before a Fall

Daisy looked up at the old **grandfather clock** in the corner of the foyer and yawned. It was twelve-thirty and there was nothing left for her to do in the office. Mrs Cartwright was supposed to have been back from her dentist's appointment by midday but there was still no sign of her, and Daisy was growing increasingly bored of waiting.

I'm sure she won't mind if I **nip** home early, she thought to herself.

She collected her few possessions from the front desk and stepped out into the bitter January wind.

| grandfather clock | Standuhr |
|---|---|
| ⚡ to nip somewhere | irgendwo hin flitzen |
| duffel coat | Winterjacke |

Pulling on her tight leather gloves, she unlocked her bicycle from the railings and began to peddle. The hood of her **duffel coat**, however, hung so low over her face that she could barely see where she was going, and a few seconds later, her bicycle was brought down to the ground with a crash.

Daisy lay for a few moments on the muddy driveway, stunned by the fall. She took a deep breath and tried to move her fingers, and then her toes. Everything still seemed to be in working order.

Slowly, she turned her head to try and see what had caused the crash: her gaze was met by two large, lifeless eyes.

**Exercise 57: Translation.** Übersetzen Sie die folgenden Sätze!

1. Daisy looked up at the old grandfather clock in boredom and yawned.

   _____

2. Mrs Cartwright was supposed to have been back from her dentist's appointment by midday, but there was no sign of her.

   _____

   _____

3. I'm sure she won't mind if I nip home early.

   _____

4. Her bicycle was brought down to the ground with a crash.

   _____

Daisy's piercing scream was heard across the road by Mavis in the post office, who dropped the pile of newspapers she had been carrying and rushed to see what had happened. As she approached the mayor's house, she saw two female figures sprawled out in the middle of the driveway. She didn't recognize the red-haired girl but her concern grew when she saw Daisy. She rushed over, lifting

| sprawled out | ausgestreckt |

Daisy's bleeding face onto the warmth of her lap.

"Oh, darling, what happened?" Mavis asked, tears filling her eyes. "Are you alright?"

"I'm fine, Aunty," came a **feeble** reply. "But I think she…" Daisy pointed to the motionless body lying next to her. "I think she…"

"It's alright, don't you worry," Mavis said calmly. "Let's sit you up and I'll go and telephone for the ambulance."

> **Exercise 58: Choose the correct alternative.** Lesen Sie weiter und unterstreichen Sie die richtige Variante!
>
> 1. Simultaneously / Meanwhile , Hudson and Constable Stawker were 2. making / taking their way back along the country roads to Glengowan.
>
> "Are you 3. planning / projecting on keeping this little fellow, 4. then / well ?" Stanley asked as Hamish jumped up from the back seat to lick the inspector's ear.
>
> "Hamish? No, no, I'm 5. bad / no good with animals. And besides, Miss Paddington would kill me." Hudson chuckled, 6. pictures / imagining Miss Paddington's face if he returned to London with the muddy terrier.

"That's a shame, sir; I think he likes you."
They sat in silence for a few moments while Stanley searched for something else to say.

"I've never caught a murderer before, Inspector. It's all quite exciting, isn't it?"

feeble — schwach

Hudson nodded, keeping his eyes on the road ahead.

"You do think we've got the right man, don't you?"

"To be honest, Stanley, that same question has been **niggling** me all morning. I think something's missing from the equation…"

"But Cartwright's got such a strong motive. Willy witnessed him planning the holiday resort on the shore of Loch Ness, wrote about it in his diary, and was killed before he could tell anyone else. John found the notes when he went to feed Hamish and tried to confront the mayor, who killed him, too. It all makes perfect sense!"

"Yes, I know," Hudson murmured hesitantly. "But something's still bothering me, I just can't work out what… I mean, we still don't know why Gregor's name is mentioned so often in the diary. And the car Gregor saw on the night of Willy's death was silver…"

"But the mayor's car is red," Stanley finished Hudson's sentence for him. "I see what you're getting at, Inspector."

"What is it that we're failing to see, Constable?" Hudson asked pensively.

"I don't know, sir," Stanley replied, shaking his head. "But if anyone can find out, it's you."

The two policemen sat in silence for a few moments longer while Hudson quietly **mused** over the case. His train of thought was suddenly disrupted, however, by a loud vibration in his coat pocket. Hudson groaned.

"Who is it, sir?" Stanley asked politely.

"It's Fergus. You answer it for me."

"But I'm driving…"

"Well pull over, I don't want to talk to him."

| to niggle | nörgeln |
|---|---|
| to muse | nachgrübeln |

Stanley stopped the car and listened attentively before hanging up.

| accelerator | Gaspedal |
| paramedic | Rettungsassistent |

"Well? What did he want? I'm not taking him back on the case, if that's what he's after."

"No, sir. There's been an accident outside the mayor's house. He thinks it would be best if we go and have a look. He said you probably wouldn't want him getting involved."

"I was worried something like this might happen…," Hudson's voice trailed off as Stanley pushed his foot down on the **accelerator**.

---

**Exercise 59: Passive voice.** Formulieren Sie die Sätze im Passiv!

1. That question has been niggling Hudson all morning.
   _____

2. Willy witnessed the mayor planning the holiday resort.
   _____

3. Stanley finished Hudson's sentence for him.
   _____

4. I'm not taking him back on the case.
   _____

---

Twenty minutes later, they were standing between two ambulances and a crowd of onlookers in the mayor's driveway. Two **paramedics** were carefully lifting Una Breannan into the back of one of the ambulances. Hudson walked up to them.

"Is she dead?" he asked.

"No, Inspector," replied the senior medic. "Just unconscious."

| to recount | erzählen |
| to talk shop | über die Arbeit reden |

"What happened to her?"

"Looks like she was run over."

"By a bicycle?" Hudson asked in disbelief.

"No, sir," the paramedic laughed. "The cold hasn't got to her yet, so she can't have been lying here for more than half an hour before Daisy bumped into her."

Hudson nodded and walked inside the house, where Mavis was consoling a traumatized Daisy.

"Miss Malden," Hudson said, greeting the sobbing young woman.

He began to ask her about the afternoon's events and, between sobs, she recounted everything she could remember.

"And you'd never seen the woman before now?"

"No, Inspector Hudson."

"Do you have any idea what she wanted to talk to Mr Cartwright about?"

"No, sir. She gave me a business card but the mayor isn't in any position to be talking shop right now, so I threw it away."

"Will that be all now, Inspector?" Mavis asked, wrapping a blanket around Daisy's shaking shoulders.

"Yes, yes, go and get her home. Your injuries aren't serious, I hope?"

**Phrasal Verbs mit get**
Das umgangssprachliche **to get to sb.** bedeutet „jmd. in Mitleidenschaft ziehen" oder „jmd. an die Nieren gehen".
Weitere Phrasal Verbs:
get at sb. — jmd. kritisieren
get back at sb. — sich an jmd. rächen

"No, just a few bumps and scratches, nothing a nice hot bath won't take care of," Mavis answered in her motherly tone.

"Very well. Take good care of yourself, Daisy."

**Exercise 60: Correct the mistakes.** Lesen Sie weiter und korrigieren Sie die sechs Fehler!

As they get up to enter, Hudson called for Constable Stawker.
"Help me look through the bins, will you, Stanley? There shall be a pink business card here somebody. It might help us further."
Stanley's head disappeared for a moment under the reception desc.
"I've got it, sir!" he called out. "Ms Una Breannan from MacGregor Developments, Edinburgh."
Hudson **cocked his head inquisitively** to a side.
"MacGregor?"
"Yes, sir. Una Breannan, MacGregor Devel…"
"Allright, thank you, Stanley," Hudson motioned for him to stop.

1. _____ 2. _____
3. _____ 4. _____
5. _____ 6. _____

He walked over to the window and peered out onto the bustling driveway.
"The notes in Willy's burnt diary pages must have read Mac Gregor, not Gregor…" Hudson muttered to himself. Then, more **audibly**, "We've been fol-

| | |
|---|---|
| to cock one's head | den Kopf schief legen |
| inquisitively | neugierig |
| audibly | hörbar |

lowing a false lead, Constable! What else do we know about this Ms Breannan?"

"The paramedics have left her belongings over there for you to **give them the once-over**," Stanley replied, pointing to a large, white plastic bag in the doorway.

| ⚡ to give sth. the once-over | etw. inspizieren |
|---|---|
| briefcase | Aktenkoffer |
| wad | Bündel |
| scuff marks *pl* | Farbspuren |
| to be on the loose | frei herumlaufen |

Hudson walked over and fished out a grey coat and a heavy black **briefcase** from the bag.

"Looks like she tried to use it as a shield against the car," Stanley said, pointing at the battered leather case.

The sides were so badly damaged that the locks had sprung open of their own accord. Hudson quickly peered inside. He lifted out a **wad** of paper and began to read.

"What does it say, sir?"

"It's a contract between Mayor Cartwright and MacGregor Developments, finalizing details of a holiday resort on Loch Ness…"

"Go on."

"Mayor Cartwright… MC. Those are the initials I've been looking for!"

Hudson closed the briefcase again and inspected the exterior. It was covered in scratches from the impact, and traces of silver paint were clear to see along the **scuff marks**."

Stanley looked up at the inspector.

"Do you think…," Stanley hesitated.

Hudson stared at him impatiently.

"Do you think we've got it all wrong?"

Hudson could see the fear in Stawker's eyes.

"I'm beginning to think so, Constable. Looks like our killer might still **be on the loose**."

| ⚡ long shot | Schuss ins Blaue |

Hudson took out his mobile and began to dial.

"Hazel? Yes, Hudson here. Look, I've got another favour to ask…" Hudson quickly brought the Superintendent up to date on the events of the past few days while she listened intently.

"A silver car you say? And the incident took place at around 11:45 a.m.? They can't be that far by now, not with all this snow on the roads. I'll alert all officers within a 50-mile radius to pull in any silver cars… Though I must admit, James, it's a long shot."

"Thank you, Hazel, I knew I could rely on you."

"By the way, what makes you think the driver's female?"

"Just a hunch," the inspector replied secretively and hung up.

**Exercise 61: Questions about the text.** Beantworten Sie die Fragen zum Text!

1. What happens to the level of Hudson's voice as he speaks?

   _____

2. In what way have the paramedics thought ahead?

   _____

3. How had Ms Breannan supposedly tried to protect herself against the oncoming car?

   _____

4. Why do Hudson and Constable Stawker think they have the wrong killer?

   _____

Fergus, unable to participate in the action, had returned to the Loch Inn for lunch. He was sitting at the kitchen table, **lamenting** to Dorothy about the poor state of his

| | |
|---|---|
| to lament | klagen |
| to go into labour | die Wehen bekommen |
| pager | Funkrufempfänger |
| rolling | sanft geschwungen |

marriage, when the telephone rang shrilly in the hallway.

"I won't be a second, son, just let me just see who that is."

Moments later, she came rushing back in, grinning widely.

"That was Duncan! Morag's **gone into labour**, but he's got a flat tyre and can't get to the hospital. He asked if you could give him a lift."

"Mum, I'm eating. Can't he go with someone else?"

"Come on, Fergus. I said you'd be there in five minutes."

Fergus grumbled to himself as he got back into his police car. The red light on the **pager** attached to his dashboard was flashing, and he threw a cursory glance over the message as he buckled his seatbelt. He read something about silver cars but, being officially off duty, paid little attention.

It wasn't long before he and Duncan were travelling along Glengowan's **rolling** hills towards the county hospital.

"Can't you go any faster?" Duncan urged, squirming with excitement in his seat.

"Don't worry, Duncan, we'll be there in a minute. Know what it is yet?"

"It's going to be a boy! A little Duncan Junior to take over his father's business one day."

Fergus was no good at this sort of talk and was grateful to see the hospital come into view. Just as they pulled into the car park, however, he saw a silver sports car tear through the exit and skid onto the main road.

"Looks like they're in a bit of a hurry," Duncan laughed.

Fergus paused and stopped the car.

"Afraid I'll have to let you out here, Duncan. I think Hudson could do with my help."

"What are you on about, lad? Come on, just drive me to the entrance and I'll…"

But Fergus had already bundled him out onto the pavement and was turning the car around. Speeding off through the snowy streets, he called headquarters for backup.

**Exercise 62: If-clauses.** Bringen Sie die Wörter in die richtige Reihenfolge, um if-Sätze zu bilden!

1. allowed | Fergus | have | he | would | action | participated | in | the | beenvif had | to

2. tyre | could | he | Duncan | driven | flat | if | had | a | himself | not | had | have

3. paid | duty | if | on | Fergus | he | been | have | attention | would | more | had

**4.** would | the | Duncan | Fergus | have | silver | driven | not | not | spotted | had | if | he | car

_____

_____


While Duncan raced through the hospital corridor to the labour ward, Hudson had also arrived and was being directed to Una Breannan's ward.

He tapped on the door before entering. She lay, frail and fatigued, beneath the pale green covers of the hospital bed. Hudson pulled up a chair and delicately touched her hand.

"Miss Breannan," Hudson whispered. "If you're feeling strong enough, I'd like to ask you some questions about the accident."

"Accident?" her voice croaked quietly. "That was no accident, Inspector, the bitch tried to kill me."

"Who? And what makes you so certain she wanted to kill you?" Hudson asked.

Una tried to sit up a little.

"I had an appointment with Quentin. He wasn't there so I left, and that's when she came driving up the path to the house. She took one look at me and started calling me all sorts of names: slut, whore, marriage-wrecker… You name it. She kept going on about me stealing her husband, and when I tried to run away she came at me with her car. I'm lucky I'm not dead."

"Indeed," Hudson said, taking a deep breath. "Can you describe the woman, or perhaps her car?"

| | |
|---|---|
| slut | Schlampe |
| wrecker | Saboteur, Zerstörer |

"It's all still very fuzzy, but she must have been in her mid-forties, with shortish brown hair. Drove a silver sports car – I won't forget that sight in a hurry, I can assure you."

"That's very helpful, Miss Breannan. And just one more question about your relationship to Mr Cartwright… It was purely business?"

"Yes," Una said, a little offended. "I'm not that sort of woman, if that's what you're thinking. We've spent a lot of time together over the past weeks, planning the holiday resort, but there was never anything else."

"I'm sorry, Miss Breannan, but I have to ask," Hudson said with a friendly smile. "Perhaps you could tell me some more about MacGregor…"

Hudson was interrupted by one of the nurses.

"Time's up, Inspector. We need to take Miss Breannan through to X-ray now."

Hudson obliged with a polite nod and wished Una a swift recovery.

Outside the hospital, Hudson took out his mobile.

"Hazel, it's me again. Look, I've made a terrible mistake. We need to find the mayor's wife, Caitlin Cartwright, immediately. I think I've solved our mystery."

> **Headquarters** endet immer auf **-s**, das nachfolgende Verb kann im Singular oder Plural stehen.
> Headquarters is/are in Rome.

There was a brief moment of silence before Hazel replied.

"If you'd like to make your way over to headquarters, Inspector Hudson, you'll find Mrs Cartwright waiting in the interrogation room."

"But how…?"

Hudson wasn't able to finish his question; Hazel had already put down the receiver.

**Exercise 63: Prepositions.** Lesen Sie weiter und ergänzen Sie den Text mit den fehlenden Präpositionen!

It was growing dark **1.** _____ the time Hudson reached the police headquarters **2.** _____ Inverness. He rushed **3.** _____ the long corridors **4.** _____ the interrogation room, only **5.** _____ see Fergus sitting patiently outside. "What are you doing here?" Hudson asked, bemused. "I caught her speeding **6.** _____ of the hospital… She's in no good state, Inspector. She half-confessed in the car **7.** _____ the way here. I don't think you'll have much trouble with her."

Hudson patted Fergus on the shoulder.
"Thank you, Sergeant Murdoch. I owe you one."
Hudson unlocked the door and entered. He was met by a hysterical, weeping woman.
"So, Mrs Cartwright," Hudson began. "It seems as though you have something to tell me."
Caitlin stared up at him, choking on her own tears.
"Or perhaps I should tell you a little story instead? One about a jealous woman, who mistook her husband's secrecy for **adultery** and **lashed out** on those around her in revenge. Am I close?"

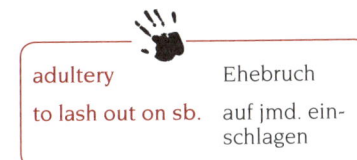

| adultery | Ehebruch |
| to lash out on sb. | auf jmd. einschlagen |

| What cheek! | Was für eine Frechheit! |
|---|---|
| sordid | schmutzig |
| audacity | Verwegenheit |

He waited to see what effect his words would have on her. Caitlin sunk her head in defeat.

"They all knew about it… I couldn't let them ruin my marriage. Willy was the first. He came up to me at the Burns Supper, saying he wanted to talk to me about my husband. What cheek! I couldn't let him blab to anyone else… I told him to wait for me outside, and…"

"I see," Hudson replied quietly. "And John?"

"He was just the same. Apparently Willy recorded Quentin's sordid affair with that MacGregor woman in some diary and he came to show it to me… I'm a proud woman, Mr Hudson. All of the villagers look up to me, I can't have people ruining everything for me."

"But murder, Mrs Cartwright? Surely there was no need…"

"Shut up!" she yelled back at him. "You have no idea what it's like being a woman in my position!"

Hudson didn't bother to retaliate as the woman was clearly out of her mind.

"And what about poor Una? What had she done?"

"Poor Una!" Caitlin yelled in disbelief. "She's the one who started all of this. She had the audacity to come to my house; she had it coming."

"I see, Mrs Cartwright, you're a proud woman. But let's, for argument's sake, say that your husband is a respectable and faithful man, who, instead of cheating on you, was planning a development project that would have made the both of you very wealthy indeed."

Caitlin looked at him, open-mouthed, while Hudson explained.

"In conclusion, however," he ended, "I'm sure the villagers might even be grateful to you for getting all this out in the open. From what I've heard, they wouldn't have been happy about the resort at all." Caitlin fainted in her chair before Hudson could officially carry out the arrest, and he exited the interrogation room, leaving the other officers to deal with her.

turmoil — Getümmel

### Exercise 64: Translation quiz. Übersetzen Sie und enträtseln Sie das Lösungswort!

1. darunter
2. verhören
3. Bauprojekt
4. teilnehmen
5. Ehebruch
6. Spur
7. wohlhabend

Lösung:

Fergus was still sitting outside.
"Thank you again, Sergeant," Hudson said. "I couldn't have done it without you."
Fergus smiled and gestured for the inspector to follow him to his car. They drove through the dark, snowy streets, while Hudson drifted in and out of sleep, exhausted after the day's turmoil. Just as they pulled up outside the Loch Inn, Hudson's mobile rang.
"Ah, Miss Paddington!" he sighed. "How are you?"

"Hello, Inspector," came her chirpy voice. "I was just wondering what time I should collect you from the station tomorrow."

"Tomorrow? Goodness, the time's flown by."

"Time flies when you're having fun, Inspector. I'm glad you've been relaxing: Sir Reginald has a new case for you to get started on as soon as possible, and it sounds difficult."

"Wonderful," Hudson replied, making no effort to hide the irony in his voice. "Thank you, Miss Paddington. Pick me up at four," he said, before hanging up.

Fergus opened the car door to let Hudson out, and the two men trudged up the snowy path to the hotel one last time.

# Final Test

**Exercise 1: Unscramble the events.** Bringen Sie die Geschehnisse in die richtige Reihenfolge!

**a)** The sides were so badly damaged that the locks had sprung open of their own accord, and Hudson was quick to peer inside. He lifted out a wad of paper and began to read.

**b)** The snow was falling heavily as Abraham dropped Hudson off outside the village post office. The little bell above the door rang as he stepped onto the doormat and brushed the snow off his shoes.

**c)** The doors slammed shut behind him, and the inspector squeezed along the aisle of the crowded train into a small compartment by the window.

**d)** Their eyes briefly met, and Hudson watched as the shiny white milk bottle slipped from Gregor's hands and landed with a crash on the wooden floor.

| 1 | 2 | 3 | 4 |
|---|---|---|---|
|   |   |   |   |

**Exercise 2: Phrasal verbs.** Bilden Sie Phrasal Verbs und ordnen Sie die passende Definition zu!

1. ☐ get back _____ a) trust in
2. ☐ talk _____ b) discuss
3. ☐ enter the _____ c) discuss thoroughly
4. ☐ count _____ d) take revenge on
5. ☐ ask _____ e) participate wholeheartedly

**Exercise 3: Say it again.** Schreiben Sie die Sätze neu und benutzen Sie die vorgegebenen Wörter!

1. This is Hudson's first holiday for a long time. hasn't

2. Hudson and Hazel once worked together in Scotland Yard. employ

3. Gregor borrowed a fair amount of money from John. lend

4. Fergus occasionally withheld the truth from the inspector. tell

5. Caitlin was about to faint. verge

**Exercise 4: Translation quiz.** Übersetzen und enträtseln Sie das Lösungswort!

1. entgegenkommend  __ __ __ __ ☐ __ __ __
2. Pfeife  __ __ __ __ ☐ __ __
3. verdächtig  __ ☐ __ __ __ __ __ __
4. Kulisse  __ __ ☐ __ __ __ __
5. Markise  ☐ __ __ __ __
6. Garderobe  __ __ __ __ ☐ __ __ __
7. überfüllt  __ __ __ __ __ ☐ __

Lösung: ☐☐☐☐☐☐☐

**Exercise 5: Who said what?** Erinnern Sie sich, wer was gesagt hat? Ordnen Sie zu!

1. ☐ "Anyone would think you were a police officer!"
2. ☐ "A terrible business. Let me just take a look at the records."
3. ☐ "You chose a fine day to visit."
4. ☐ "Nor would you in his situation."

a) Abraham Darling
b) Mavis Leary
c) Cordelia Conall
d) Quentin Cartwright

**Exercise 6: Unscramble.** Bringen Sie die Buchstaben in die richtige Reihenfolge!

1. sdncire       _____
2. sonuanyom     _____
3. rsteqrahadue  _____
4. spfgierntrni  _____

**Exercise 7: Word search.** Finden Sie die sieben Berufe aus der Geschichte!

| P | E | R | Z | T | B | R | O | O | L | S |
|---|---|---|---|---|---|---|---|---|---|---|
| A | G | I | H | Y | U | G | D | E | E | E |
| T | I | K | O | N | S | K | C | A | J | C |
| H | O | U | S | E | K | E | E | P | E | R |
| O | A | G | I | H | E | M | O | O | M | E |
| L | D | K | F | A | R | M | E | R | N | T |
| O | C | K | O | J | K | E | W | Y | U | A |
| G | S | O | F | F | I | C | E | R | T | R |
| I | X | Q | S | H | D | G | B | V | E | Y |
| S | A | L | A | N | D | L | A | D | Y | R |
| T | R | A | V | U | M | E | P | A | E | I |

# Answers

**Exercise 1:** 1. gestured 2. inspector 3. wonderful 4. nervous 5. commuter 6. swiftly 7. majestic

**Exercise 2:** 1. Now departing from platform 1 is the 8:06 train to Inverness.
2. I'm going to visit my grandchildren.
3. It had been a hectic morning.
4. The old lady continued to chat away.

**Exercise 3:** 1. Because othe old lady had knitted a long, yellow scarf.
2. Because he was in need of a good rest.
3. Because of the strong wind and biting cold.
4. No. Inspector Hudson was going to find a taxi himself.

**Exercise 4:** 1. die Zündung 2. er murmelte 3. eine Touristenfalle 4. Ruhe und Frieden

**Exercise 5:** 1. meet 2. having 3. feel 4. followed

**Exercise 6:** 1. As he approached 2. happy voices 3. through 4. at least 5. by the looks of it 6. out of place 7. looking forward to

**Exercise 7:** 1. traditional 2. almighty 3. Scottish 4. stocky 5. bright-red 6. Fantastic 7. real 8. nearing

**Exercise 8:**

| L | T | A | R | T | A | N | L |
|---|---|---|---|---|---|---|---|
| H | E | N | A | A | O | E | O |
| A | Z | D | U | T | E | E | C |
| G | U | K | H | T | I | P | H |
| G | X | I | Q | I | N | S | N |
| I | L | L | F | E | E | W | E |
| S | O | T | K | S | H | A | S |
| B | A | G | P | I | P | E | S |

**Exercise 9:** 1. eventually 2. breathe 3. unfamiliar 4. draw

**Exercise 10:** 1. rose 2. crept 3. make 4. sleeping 5. was sitting 6. were

**Exercise 11:** 1. False. Fergus does not know Hudson is police inspector. 2. True. 3. False. Fergus doubts there will be an investigation. 4. False. Hudson is unable to stop thinking about the case.

**Exercise 12:** 1. feeling 2. always 3. knocked 4. brings 5. years 6. like 7. once

**Exercise 13:** 1. keenness; keenly 2. strength; strongly 3. knowledge; knowingly 4. sparkle; sparklingly

**Exercise 14:** 1. lucky Willy 2. sad 3. a little 4. thin

**Exercise 15:** 1. followed 2. corridor 3. materials 4. square 5. luxuriously

**Exercise 16:**

| 1 R | 2 E | 3 C | 4 O | 5 R | 6 D | 7 S | 8 W |
|---|---|---|---|---|---|---|---|
| 22 E | 23 L | 24 L | 25 S | 26 P | 27 O | 28 K | 9 I |
| 21 W | 36 H | 37 I | 38 S | 39 K | 40 Y | 29 E | 10 R |
| 20 O | 35 W | 34 O | 33 R | 32 R | 31 A | 30 N | 11 L |
| 19 N | 18 S | 17 S | 16 E | 15 L | 14 E | 13 F | 12 I |

**Exercise 17:** 1. Während des Abendessens war die Atmosphäre ziemlich ungemütlich.
2. Fergus weigerte sich, die anderen Gäste wahrzunehmen.
3. In sicherer Entfernung von den neugierigen Ohren der anderen Gäste entschuldigte sich Hudson.

**Exercise 18:** 1. may 2. informed 3. half 4. around 5. within

**Exercise 19:** 1. The inspector's hand was shaken.
2. Hudson was handed a green folder.
3. A brief statement was given.
4. The glasses were raised.

**Exercise 20:** 1. 12:15 a.m. 2. past 3. it's 4. between 5. before 6. notice

**Exercise 21:** 1. He wasn't one for parties.
2. No, he kept himself to himself.
3. He rarely leaves the village; Mrs MacDougal can give him a lift.
4. He doesn't pry into other people's business.

**Exercise 22:** 1. If Hudson had left his mobile on, he would have been disturbed.
2. If Hudson wants to know more, he must meet Fergus at the pub.
3. If the pathologist has any results, she will contact Hudson.
4. If Hudson returns home empty-handed, Miss Paddington may be disappointed.

**Exercise 23:** 1. down 2. from 3. out 4. behind 5. from

**Exercise 24:** 1. placate 2. obliterate 3. crunch 4. chime 5. unravel 6. gruesome 7. unmistakable 8. skein
**Lösung:** Loch Ness

**Exercise 25:** 1. to stop himself 2. finding out 3. walking up 4. silently 5. echoing 6. waiting for

**Exercise 26:** 1. ... handed over the scrunched-up papers. 2. ... would have heard the yelling. 3. ... he not been paralyzed by pain. 4. Hudson would have carried on sleeping ...

**Exercise 27:** 1. pointed to 2. I'd say 3. by a blow 4. shaking his head 5. walked around 6. to the mortuary 7. at the moment

**Exercise 28:** 1. skips 2. unattended 3. smelly 4. apart from 5. beamed

**Exercise 29:** 1. Fergus asked Hudson to step outside for a moment.
2. Hudson demanded to know what Fergus wanted.
3. Hudson speculated that they had a serial murderer on their hands.

**4.** The inspector requested that Fergus came with him to the wool mill first.

**Exercise 30:** Hudson nickte Sergeant Murdoch auffordernd zu und riss ihm ein Stück Tartan-stoff ab. Sofort machten sich die Polizisten auf den Weg zum Lagerhaus, in dem die Stoffballen gelagert wurden.

„Ich kann Ihnen aber gleich sagen", meinte Morag, während sie den braunen Tartan zwischen ihren Fingern rieb, „so etwas wie das hier werden Sie in unserer Spinnerei nicht finden."

„Und wieso nicht?", fragte Hudson skeptisch.

**Exercise 31:** 
1. The women's round stomachs.
2. They kept them in for observation.
3. The policemen's cars.
4. The tartans' colours vary.

**Exercise 32:**

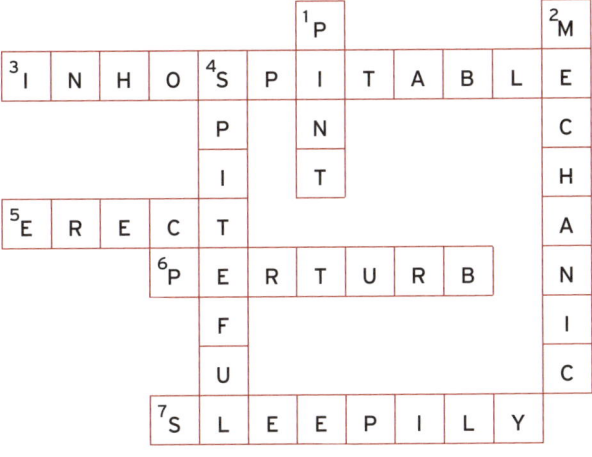

**Exercise 33:** 1. fishy 2. found 3. match 4. blankly

**Exercise 34:** 1. could 2. stepped 3. was due 4. was 5. Help yourself 6. will be ready 7. Is

**Exercise 35:** 1. Divorce is a messy business.
2. Just the man I wanted to see.
3. He smiled with as much good cheer as he could muster.
4. Why on earth didn't you tell me?

**Exercise 36:** 1. b 2. d 3. a 4. c

**Exercise 37:** 1. Willy died accidentally.
2. Hudson was thinking deeply.
3. The inspector glanced uneasily at the body.
4. Hudson happily left the mortuary.

**Exercise 38:** 1. driveway 2. badge 3. rummaging 4. explaining 5. bumped 6. boot/luggage compartment lid

**Exercise 39:** 1. a 2. b 3. b 4. b

**Exercise 40:**

| S | I | L | W | E | M | U | R | D | E | R |
|---|---|---|---|---|---|---|---|---|---|---|
| E | T | R | A | Q | D | N | F | A | I | E |
| R | A | X | R | F | I | H | O | N | X | V |
| G | R | U | R | O | F | B | R | Q | P | I |
| E | S | T | A | T | E | M | E | N | T | D |
| A | E | G | N | T | A | A | N | I | O | E |
| N | L | K | T | E | L | I | S | S | M | N |
| T | P | V | O | W | A | J | I | L | D | C |
| O | C | R | I | M | E | S | C | E | N | E |

**Exercise 41:** 1. saliva 2. remorse 3. report 4. mismatched

Exercise 42: **1.** idea **2.** complicated **3.** afternoon **4.** mentioned **5.** connection **6.** aware **7.** heard

Exercise 43: **1.** True **2.** False. Jessie is still a suspect. **3.** True **4.** True

Exercise 44: **1.** perceptive **2.** binoculars **3.** plumped **4.** creaked **5.** anxious **6.** sightings

Exercise 45: **1.** interest; interestingly **2.** intent/intention; intentionally **3.** anger; angrily **4.** obedience; obediently

Exercise 46: **1.** stopped **2.** go **3.** was waiting **4.** rang **5.** peered **6.** Looks

Exercise 47: **1.** Hudson finds the presence of Gregor's name in the diary suspicious.
**2.** Hudson climbed in through the window before letting the officers in.
**3.** The inspector was not told that two of his main suspects were having an affair.
**4.** Fergus is taken off the case before he is arrested as well.

Exercise 48:

| 1 I | 2 N | 3 D | 4 I | 5 S | 6 C | 7 R | 8 E |
|---|---|---|---|---|---|---|---|
| 24 M | 25 P | 26 A | 27 T | 28 H | 29 E | 30 T | 9 E |
| 23 Y | 40 L | 41 D | 42 E | 43 R | 44 U | 31 I | 10 T |
| 22 S | 39 U | 48 R | 47 U | 46 O | 45 M | 32 C | 11 H |
| 21 D | 38 O | 37 H | 36 S | 35 D | 34 L | 33 O | 12 E |
| 20 N | 19 U | 18 O | 17 P | 16 A | 15 Y | 14 R | 13 O |

Exercise 49: **1.** bellowed **2.** had **3.** replied vehemently

|  |  |
|---|---|
|  | **4.** shivering **5.** freezing **6.** cleared his throat **7.** switching on |
| **Exercise 50:** | **1.** … he is in possession of the blowpipe? **2.** … he hadn't placed some unlucky debts. **3.** … see if he still has the keys to the mayor's house. **4.** Gregor wouldn't have stolen from the petty cash, … |
| **Exercise 51:** | **1.** it all happened **2.** I remember **3.** whispered something **4.** It seems **5.** can **6.** his decision **7.** course of action |
| **Exercise 52:** | **1.** pulled into (enter) **2.** contentedly (comfortably) **3.** baggage (belongings) **4.** unsuspecting (unwary) |
| **Exercise 53:** | **1.** Stanley asked if Mr Cartwright would like to come with him. **2.** The mayor angrily asked if they were arresting him. **3.** The mayor shouted back that he didn't even know that John was dead. **4.** Stanley's voice echoed that Inspector Hudson thought it might be more convenient. |
| **Exercise 54:** | Ein paar Meilen entfernt in der Glengowan Wollspinnerei lehnte sich kurze Zeit später Mrs MacDougal schläfrig in ihrem heißen Schaumbad zurück. Duncan kam rein und setzte sich auf den Rand der vollen Wanne. „Was machen die Rückenschmerzen, Schatz?", fragte er und massierte ihre feuchten Schultern. „Ein bisschen besser, Liebling", sagte Morag. Sie stieg aus dem Bad und hüllte sich in ein großes blaues Handtuch. |

**Exercise 55:** 1. b 2. d 3. a 4. c

**Exercise 56:**

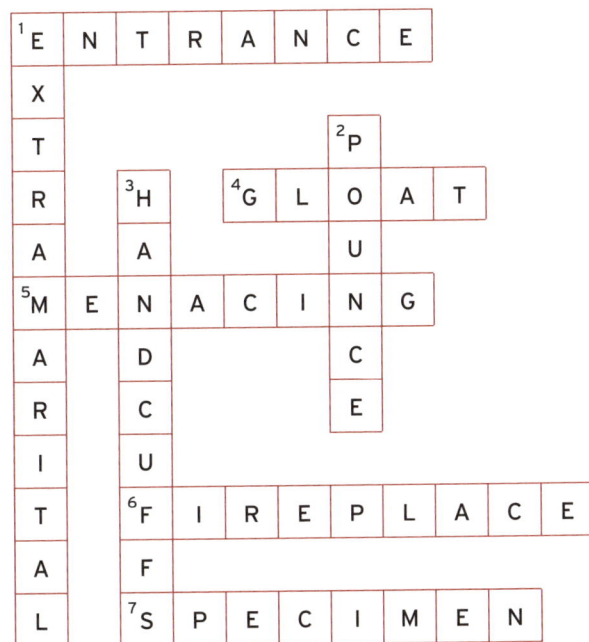

**Exercise 57:** 1. Gelangweilt schaute Dasiy zur Standuhr und gähnte.
2. Mrs Cartwright hätte eigentlich mittags von ihrem Zahnarzttermin zurück sein sollen, aber es war keine Spur von ihr zu sehen.
3. Ich bin sicher, sie hat nichts dagegen, wenn ich früher nach Hause flitze.
4. Ihr Fahrrad wurde krachend zu Fall gebracht.

**Exercise 58:** 1. Meanwhile 2. making 3. planning 4. then 5. no good 6. imagining

**Exercise 59:** 1. Hudson has been niggled by that question all morning.

2. The mayor was witnessed planning the holiday resort.
3. Hudson's sentence was finished for him.
4. He won't be taken back on the case.

Exercise 60: 1. got 2. should 3. somewhere 4. desk
5. to one side 6. alright

Exercise 61: 1. It becomes more audible.
2. They have left Ms Breannan's belongings ready for the inspector to look at.
3. She used her briefcase as a shield.
4. Because the mayor is still under arrest and another attempted murder has occurred.

Exercise 62: 1. If Fergus had been allowed to, he would have participated in the action.
2. If Duncan had not had a flat tyre, he could have driven himself.
3. If he had been on duty, Fergus would have paid more attention.
4. If Fergus had not driven Duncan, he would not have spotted the silver car.

Exercise 63: 1. by 2. in 3. through/along 4. to/towards
5. to 6. out 7. on

Exercise 64: 1. beneath 2. interrogate 3. development
4. participate 5. adultery 6. trace 7. wealthy
**Lösung:** holiday

# Final Test

**Exercise 1:** 1. c 2. b 3. d 4. a

**Exercise 2:** 1. get back at; d 2. talk through; c 3. enter the spirit; e 4. count on; a 5. ask after; b

**Exercise 3:** 1. Hudson hasn't been on holiday for a long time. 2. Hudson and Hazel were once both employed by Scotland Yard. 3. John lent a fair amount of money to Gregor. 4. Fergus did not always tell the inspector the truth. 5. Caitlin was on the verge of fainting.

**Exercise 4:** 1. oncoming 2. blowpipe 3. suspicious 4. setting 5. awning 6. cloakroom 7. crowded
**Lösung:** mistake

**Exercise 5:** 1. b 2. d 3. a 4. c

**Exercise 6:** 1. cinders 2. anonymous 3. headquarters 4. fingerprints

**Exercise 7:**

| P | E | R | Z | T | B | R | O | O | L | S |
|---|---|---|---|---|---|---|---|---|---|---|
| A | G | I | H | Y | U | G | D | E | E | E |
| T | I | K | O | N | S | K | C | A | J | C |
| H | O | U | S | E | K | E | E | P | E | R |
| O | A | G | I | H | E | M | O | O | M | E |
| L | D | K | F | A | R | M | E | R | N | T |
| O | C | K | O | J | K | E | W | Y | U | A |
| G | S | O | F | F | I | C | E | R | T | R |
| I | X | Q | S | H | D | G | B | V | E | Y |
| S | A | L | A | N | D | L | A | D | Y | R |
| T | R | A | V | U | M | E | P | A | E | I |

# Glossary

↯ = umgangssprachlich
Scot = schottisch

| | |
|---|---|
| A&E (Accident & Emergency) | Notaufnahme |
| abundance | Fülle, Vielzahl |
| accelerator | Gaspedal |
| adamantly | unerbittlich |
| adultery | Ehebruch |
| ↯ a few bob | ziemlich viel Geld |
| aisle | Gang, Mittelgang |
| ajar | angelehnt |
| array | große Anzahl |
| audacity | Verwegenheit |
| audibly | hörbar |
| Auld Lang Syne (Scot) | wörtl. "die gute alte Zeit", ein bekanntes schottisches Lied, verfasst von Burns |
| austere | karg |
| awning | Markise |
| aye (Scot) | ja |
| babble | Geplapper, Murmeln |
| backlog | Arbeitsrückstand |
| bagpipes *pl* | Dudelsack |
| banisters *pl* | Treppengeländer |

| | |
|---|---|
| battered | zusammengeschlagen |
| to beam | strahlen |
| to be apalled by sth. | über etw. entsetzt sein |
| to bear with sb. | mit jmd. Geduld haben |
| to beckon | jmd. heranwinken |
| bedraggled | ungepflegt |
| begrudgingly | widerwillig |
| ⚡ to be in good nick | top in Schuss sein |
| to bellow | bellen, grölen |
| bemused | verwirrt |
| to be on the loose | frei herumlaufen |
| to be out of touch with sth. | den Kontakt verloren haben zu |
| to be taken aback | aus der Fassung gebracht sein |
| ⚡ to be rolling in it | sehr reich sein |
| bewilderment | Verwirrung |
| bin-liner | Müllbeutel |
| to bleach | ausbleichen |
| bleating | Geblöke |
| blizzard | Schneesturm |
| blow pipe | Blasrohr |
| to blurt sth. out | etw. ausschwatzen |
| blush | Schamröte |
| bob | *hier*: Pagenkopf |
| bonnet | Motorhaube |
| to brace oneself | sich auf etw. gefasst machen |
| breadth | Umfang |
| ⚡ brew | Tee |
| briefcase | Aktenkoffer |
| brimming | bis zum Rande gefüllt |
| brisk | flott |
| brooding | grüblerisch |
| bubbly | quirlig |
| to bundle sb. into sth. | jmd. verfrachten in |

| | |
|---|---|
| Burns Night | Geburtstag des schottischen Dichters Robert Burns |
| Burns Supper | in Schottland ein jährliches Fest zu Ehren des Dichters Robert Burns |
| busker | Straßenmusikant |
| busybody | Topfgucker |
| to call it a night | Schluss machen |
| carved | geschnitzt |
| cassock | Soutane |
| to catch wind of sth. | etw. kapieren |
| CCTV camera | Videoüberwachungssystem |
| charred | verkohlt |
| to chime | läuten |
| chirpy | munter |
| chitchat | Geplauder |
| chugging | Tuckern |
| cinder | Asche |
| to clack | klappern |
| to clamber out of sth. | aus etw. klettern |
| clan | Klan |
| clenched teeth | zusammengebissene Zähne |
| clinking | Klirren |
| cluttered | vollgestellt |
| to cock one's head | den Kopf schief legen |
| ⚡ come rain or shine | bei jedem Wetter |
| commuter | Pendler(in) |
| composure | Haltung |
| concede | einräumen, zugeben |
| to consume | *hier*: verzehren |
| contentedly | zufrieden |
| contraction | Wehe |
| to cordon sth. off | etw. absperren |
| to crackle | knistern |

| | |
|---|---|
| craftsmanship | Handwerkskunst |
| to crouch | (sich) zusammenkauern |
| crumpled | zerknautscht |
| to cup one's hand around sth. | die Hand schützend um etw. legen |
| ⚡ cuppa | Tasse Tee |
| cursory | kursorisch |
| curtly | kurz angebunden |
| to dab | tupfen |
| dashboard | Armaturenbrett |
| to decipher | entziffern |
| derelict | verfallen |
| dereliction of duty | Pflichtversäumnis |
| desolate | trostlos |
| despondent | mutlos |
| detour | Umleitung |
| disgruntled | verärgert, verstimmt |
| disheartened | entmutigt |
| dishevelled | zerzaust |
| to disperse | sich auflösen |
| distressed | erschüttert |
| to distract sb. | jmd. ablenken |
| ⚡ dog collar | Priesterkragen |
| draughty | zugig |
| to drive a hard bargain | hart verhandeln |
| drone | *hier*: Basspfeife |
| drowsily | schläfrig |
| duffel coat | Winterjacke |
| dumbstruck | sprachlos |
| dump | Müllhalde |
| dusk | Abenddämmerung |
| each to his own | jedem das Seine |
| ebony | Ebenholz |
| endearing | reizend |

| | |
|---|---|
| to engulf | umringen, verschlingen |
| to ensue | folgen |
| etched | geätzt |
| to evict sb. | jmd. rausschmeißen, jmd. auf die Straße setzen |
| extramarital | außerehelich |
| to falter | zaudern |
| feeble | schwach |
| to file for divorce | die Scheidung einreichen |
| ⚡ to fill sb. in on sth. | jmd. über etw. informieren |
| fire poker | Schüreisen |
| ⚡ to fit the bill | das Richtige sein |
| flagstone | Steinplatte |
| flock | Herde |
| to flop | hinplumpsen |
| flushed | errötet |
| flustered | aufgeregt |
| food for thought | Stoff zum Nachdenken |
| forbidding | bedrohlich |
| forensics | Gerichtsmedizin |
| four-poster bed | Himmelbett |
| four-wheel drive | Geländewagen |
| French windows *pl* | Fenstertüren |
| fuzzy | unscharf |
| gash | Schnittwunde |
| gem | Juwel |
| ⚡ to give sb. their marching orders | jmd. den Laufpass geben |
| ⚡ to give sth. the once-over | etw. inspizieren |
| to gloat | sich hämisch freuen |
| to glower | finster blicken |
| to go back a long way | sich lange kennen |
| to go into labour | die Wehen bekommen |
| grace | *hier*: Tischgebet |

| | |
|---|---|
| grandfather clock | Standuhr |
| to grimace | das Gesicht verziehen |
| grime | Schmutz |
| gruff | rau |
| haggis (Scot) | schottisches Gericht aus Schafsinnereien |
| hardened criminal | Schwerverbrecher(in) |
| haven | Oase |
| head over heels | bis über beide Ohren verliebt |
| to herd in | hüten |
| high and low | überall |
| hit-and-run | Unfall mit Fahrerflucht |
| to hover | in der Luft schweben |
| to humour sb. | jmd. seinen Willen lassen |
| hump | Buckel |
| ⚡ hunch | Ahnung |
| to hurtle | rasen |
| hustle and bustle | Hektik, Trubel |
| impeccably | makellos |
| ⚡ in a flap | aufgeregt |
| ⚡ in a huff | verärgert |
| in dismay | entsetzt |
| in leaps and bounds | in großen Sprüngen |
| to instil sth. into sb. | jmd. etw. anerziehen |
| to intervene | dazwischenfahren |
| in tow | im Schlepptau |
| in unison | gemeinsam |
| incessant | ununterbrochen |
| inconsolable | untröstlich |
| incriminating evidence | belastendes Material |
| indentation | Vertiefung |
| indiscretion | Unüberlegtheit |
| inhospitality | Unwirtlichkeit |
| innards *pl* | Innereien |

| | |
|---|---|
| inquisitively | neugierig |
| insufferable | unerträglich |
| intentional | mit Absicht |
| intently | konzentriert |
| intercom | Sprechanlage |
| intriguing | faszinierend |
| jest | Spaß |
| to jiggle | rütteln |
| jolly | fröhlich |
| to jolt sb. out of sth. | jmd. aus etw. aufrütteln |
| to keep one's eyes peeled | die Augen offen halten |
| keepsake | Andenken |
| key fact | Tatsache |
| kilt | Schottenrock |
| laddie (Scot) | Bursche |
| to lament | klagen |
| landing | *hier*: Treppenflur |
| to lash out on sb. | auf jmd. einschlagen |
| lass (Scot) | Mädel |
| to lay a fire | ein Feuer anmachen |
| legible | lesbar |
| to linger | lungern |
| log fire | Kaminfeuer |
| ⚡ long shot | Schuss ins Blaue |
| to look into sth. | etw. prüfen |
| loom | Webmaschine |
| ⚡ loopy | durchgeknallt |
| to lull sb. to sleep | jmd. in den Schlaf wiegen |
| to make a nuisance of oneself | andere belästigen |
| majestic | majestätisch |
| meekly | kleinlaut |
| menacingly | bedrohlich |
| miser | Geizhals |

| | |
|---|---|
| ↯ missus | Ehefrau |
| ↯ mite | Armer |
| morgue | Leichenhalle |
| mortgage | Hypothek |
| mound | Haufen |
| to muse | nachgrübeln |
| to muster | zusammenbringen |
| ↯ na | nein |
| neeps and tatties *pl* (Scot) | Rüben und Kartoffeln, typische Beilage zu Haggis |
| ↯ Nessie | Spitzname für das Loch Ness Monster |
| to niggle | nörgeln |
| nimble | flink |
| ↯ to nip somewhere | irgendwo hin flitzen |
| to no avail | vergebens |
| Northern Constabulary | Polizei von Nordschottland |
| ↯ nosh | Fressalien |
| novelty | *hier*: Kuriosität |
| to oblige sb. | jmd. entgegenkommen |
| to obliterate | verdecken |
| obstinate | dickköpfig |
| on cue | wie gerufen |
| on the spot | auf der Stelle |
| ornate | kunstvoll |
| outhouse | Nebengebäude |
| oven mitt | Topflappen |
| pager | Funkrufempfänger |
| paramedic | Rettungsassistent |
| parish | Pfarrbezirk |
| passerby | Passant(in) |
| ↯ peck | flüchtiger Kuss |
| penchant | Vorliebe |
| pensive | nachdenklich |

| | |
|---|---|
| to perch | hocken |
| to perturb sb. | jmd. beunruhigen |
| persuasive | konsequent |
| petty cash | Portokasse |
| pinafore | Schürze |
| piqued | pikiert |
| to placate sb. | jmd. besänftigen |
| platter | Servierteller |
| ⚡ to plop down | hinplumpsen |
| plump | füllig |
| plush | nobel |
| ⚡ poky | winzig |
| porridge | Haferbrei |
| port of call | Ziel |
| to pounce on sb. | sich auf jmd. stürzen |
| to pound sth. | auf/an etw. hämmern |
| to pout | schmollen |
| precariously | unsicher |
| premeditated | vorsätzlich |
| proceedings *pl* | Ablauf |
| process of elimination | Ausschlussverfahren |
| to prod | stupsen |
| profanity | Obszönität |
| to proffer | anbieten |
| profusely | reichlich |
| prying | neugierig |
| to puff | *hier*: aufsteigen; hinausblasen |
| puffing and panting | schnaufend und keuchend |
| racket | Lärm |
| rap | *hier*: Klopfen |
| to reciprocate | erwidern |
| to recline | sich zurücklegen |
| to recount | erzählen |
| rectory | Pfarrhaus |

| | |
|---|---|
| reluctantly | ungern, widerstrebend |
| rendition | Interpretation, Version |
| to repeal sth. | etw. widerrufen |
| to retort | antworten |
| rickety | klapprig |
| rolling | sanft geschwungen |
| rugged | rau, markant |
| to rummage | wühlen |
| rundown | Zusammenfassung |
| to scold sb. | jmd. schimpfen |
| ⚡ Scottie dog | Scottish Terrier, brit. Hunderasse |
| to scramble | *hier*: klettern |
| scrapyard | Schrottplatz |
| scrawl | Gekrakel |
| to scribble sth. | etw. hinkritzeln |
| to scrunch up one's face | das Gesicht verziehen |
| to scuffle | schlurfen |
| scuff marks *pl* | Farbspuren |
| to scurry | trippeln |
| to scuttle | hoppeln |
| search warrant | Durchsuchungsbefehl |
| seething | kochend vor Wut |
| sheepishly | kleinlaut |
| shifty | unaufrichtig |
| shock (of hair) | Haarschopf |
| shortbread | Buttergebäck |
| skein | Strang |
| skip | Schuttcontainer |
| to slump | sacken, fallen |
| ⚡ slut | Schlampe |
| snarl | Zähnefletschen |
| snug | gemütlich, kuschelig |
| sordid | schmutzig |
| specimen | Exemplar |

| | |
|---|---|
| spiteful | boshaft |
| splendid | großartig |
| sprawled out | ausgestreckt |
| to squabble | zanken |
| to squint | blinzeln, die Augen zusammenkneifen |
| | |
| staff | *hier*: Stock |
| stately | stattlich |
| to stifle | etw. unterdrücken |
| to stipulate | vertraglich festsetzen |
| stocky | untersetzt |
| stone-clad | mit Stein verkleidet |
| stretcher | Trage |
| stride | Schritt |
| sturdy | kräftig |
| submerged | unter Wasser gesetzt |
| superintendent | Hauptkommissarin |
| surge | plötzlicher Anstieg |
| surly | mürrisch |
| to swathe | einwickeln |
| to swerve | kurven |
| to take a liking to sb. | von jmd. angetan sein |
| to take sth. at face value | etw. für bare Münze nehmen |
| ⚡ to talk shop | über die Arbeit reden |
| to tamper with sth. | unerlaubte Änderungen an etw. vornehmen |
| | |
| tartan | karierter Schottenstoff |
| tattered | zerrissen |
| to teem with sth. | überfüllt mit etw. |
| tentatively | zögernd |
| ⚡ the real McCoy | der wahre Jakob, das einzig Wahre |
| | |
| till | Kasse |
| tipsily | beschwipst |

| | |
|---|---|
| to trail | schleifen |
| to trudge | mit schweren Schritten gehen |
| tumbler | Trinkglas |
| turmoil | Getümmel |
| turnip | Weisrübe |
| unbeknown to sb. | ohne jds. Wissen |
| unyielding | unnachgiebig |
| to usher in | hineinführen |
| verge | *hier*: Grünstreifen; Rand |
| vigorous | energisch |
| wad | Bündel |
| to wag one's finger at sb. | jmd. mit dem Finger drohen |
| wee (Scot) | klein |
| ⚡ wellies | Gummistiefel |
| What cheek! | Was für eine Frechheit! |
| ⚡ whopping | riesig |
| to wince | zucken |
| windy | *hier*: kurvenreich |
| wits *pl* | Verstand |
| woefully | elend |
| wool mill | Wollspinnerei |
| worse for wear | schäbig |
| wrecker | Saboteur(in), Zerstörer(in) |
| to write off | als Totalschaden deklarieren |
| to writhe | sich drehen und winden |
| to yank sth. | an etw. ziehen |
| yapping | Kläffen |
| ye (Scot) | ihr (höflich) |

# List of Exercises

|    | Focus         | Exercise                       | Page |
|----|---------------|--------------------------------|------|
| 1  | Vocabulary    | Unscramble                     | 6    |
| 2  | Grammar       | Word order                     | 8    |
| 3  | Comprehension | Questions about the text       | 10   |
| 4  | Vocabulary    | Translation                    | 12   |
| 5  | Grammar       | Verb forms                     | 13   |
| 6  | Grammar       | Correct the mistakes           | 15   |
| 7  | Grammar       | Adjectives                     | 17   |
| 8  | Vocabulary    | Hidden words                   | 19   |
| 9  | Vocabulary    | Odd one out                    | 22   |
| 10 | Vocabulary    | Verb forms                     | 23   |
| 11 | Comprehension | True or false?                 | 26   |
| 12 | Vocabulary    | Fill in the blanks             | 27   |
| 13 | Vocabulary    | Word forms                     | 28   |
| 14 | Vocabulary    | Antonyms                       | 30   |
| 15 | Vocabulary    | Unscramble                     | 31   |
| 16 | Vocabulary    | Word spiral                    | 33   |
| 17 | Vocabulary    | Translation                    | 34   |
| 18 | Grammar       | Choose the correct alternative | 35   |
| 19 | Grammar       | Passive voice                  | 37   |
| 20 | Grammar       | Correct the mistakes           | 38   |
| 21 | Comprehension | Questions about the text       | 40   |
| 22 | Grammar       | If-clauses                     | 42   |
| 23 | Grammar       | Prepositions                   | 44   |
| 24 | Vocabulary    | Translation quiz               | 47   |
| 25 | Vocabulary    | Fill in the blanks             | 50   |
| 26 | Comprehension | What would have happened?      | 52   |
| 27 | Vocabulary    | Translation                    | 54   |
| 28 | Vocabulary    | Synonyms                       | 56   |
| 29 | Grammar       | Reported speech                | 58   |
| 30 | Vocabulary    | Translation                    | 59   |
| 31 | Grammar       | Plural                         | 61   |
| 32 | Vocabulary    | Crossword puzzle               | 63   |

|    | Focus         | Exercise                       | Page |
|----|---------------|--------------------------------|------|
| 33 | Vocabulary    | Synonyms                       | 65   |
| 34 | Grammar       | Verb forms                     | 67   |
| 35 | Vocabulary    | Idiomatic expressions          | 68   |
| 36 | Comprehension | Unscramble the dialogue        | 70   |
| 37 | Grammar       | Adjectives and adverbs         | 72   |
| 38 | Vocabulary    | Translation                    | 73   |
| 39 | Grammar       | Multiple choice                | 76   |
| 40 | Vocabulary    | Hidden words                   | 78   |
| 41 | Vocabulary    | Odd one out                    | 81   |
| 42 | Vocabulary    | Fill in the blanks             | 82   |
| 43 | Comprehension | True or false?                 | 84   |
| 44 | Vocabulary    | Unscramble                     | 85   |
| 45 | Vocabulary    | Word forms                     | 87   |
| 46 | Grammar       | Verb forms                     | 88   |
| 47 | Grammar       | Unscramble the sentences       | 91   |
| 48 | Vocabulary    | Word spiral                    | 93   |
| 49 | Vocabulary    | Fill in the blanks             | 94   |
| 50 | Comprehension | What would have happened?      | 96   |
| 51 | Vocabulary    | Translation                    | 98   |
| 52 | Vocabulary    | Synonyms                       | 100  |
| 53 | Grammar       | Reported speech                | 102  |
| 54 | Vocabulary    | Translation                    | 104  |
| 55 | Vocabulary    | Match up the phrases           | 106  |
| 56 | Vocabulary    | Crossword puzzle               | 109  |
| 57 | Vocabulary    | Translation                    | 111  |
| 58 | Vocabulary    | Choose the correct alternative | 112  |
| 59 | Grammar       | Passive voice                  | 114  |
| 60 | Grammar       | Correct the mistakes           | 116  |
| 61 | Comprehension | Questions about the text       | 118  |
| 62 | Grammar       | If-clauses                     | 120  |
| 63 | Grammar       | Prepositions                   | 123  |
| 64 | Vocabulary    | Translation quiz               | 125  |

## Final Test

|   | Focus         | Exercise              | Page |
|---|---------------|-----------------------|------|
| 1 | Comprehension | Unscramble the events | 127  |
| 2 | Vocabulary    | Phrasal verbs         | 128  |
| 3 | Grammar       | Say it again          | 128  |
| 4 | Vocabulary    | Translation quiz      | 129  |
| 5 | Comprehension | Who said what?        | 129  |
| 6 | Vocabulary    | Unscramble            | 130  |
| 7 | Vocabulary    | Word search           | 130  |

# SilverLine für Schule, Studium und Beruf

## 30 Reihen | 15 Sprachen | 230 Titel

SilverLine Lernbox • SilverLine Sprachkurs einfach & aktiv • SilverLine Die Grammatik
SilverLine Wörterbücher • SilverLine Kochen auf … • SilverLine Backen auf …
SilverLine Typische Fehler • SilverLine Landeskunde • SilverLine … leicht gemacht
SilverLine Business English Trainer • SilverLine Bildwörterbuch • SilverLine Kurzgrammatik
SilverLine Express • SilverLine Sprachrätsel • SilverLine Grundwortschatz in Bildern
SilverLine Basiswortschatz • SilverLine Die 2000 wichtigsten Wörter
SilverLine Sofort sprechen • SilverLine Sprachführer für die Reise • SilverLine Update

Compact Verlag GmbH
Baierbrunner Str. 27 · 81379 München · Tel. 089/74 51 61-0 · Fax 089/75 60 95
www.compactverlag.de · www.lernkrimi.de

# Lernkrimi Lektüren Englisch

**A Cry in the Darkness**
Kurzkrimis
ISBN 978-3-8174-9984-7

**Death at Land's End**
Kurzkrimis
ISBN 978-3-8174-9658-7

**The Murderer Next Door**
Kurzkrimis
ISBN 978-3-8174-9438-5

**Blood and Breakfast**
Kurzkrimis
ISBN 978-3-8174-7760-9

**Deadly Business**
Kurzkrimis
ISBN 978-3-8174-9215-2

**It Was Murder, My Lord**
Kurzkrimis
ISBN 978-3-8174-7734-0

**Last Exit Waterloo Bridge**
Kurzkrimis
ISBN 978-3-8174-7733-3

**Murder at Teatime**
Kurzkrimis
ISBN 978-3-8174-7839-2

**Long Time No Kill**
Classic
ISBN 978-3-8174-9794-2

**Murderous Collection**
Sammelband 10 in 1
ISBN 978-3-8174-8967-1

**Bullets over Bristol**
Kurzkrimis
ISBN 978-3-8174-8544-4

**Death Comes Knocking**
Kurzkrimis
ISBN 978-3-8174-7945-0

**Murderous Network**
Kurzkrimis
ISBN 978-3-8174-9312-8

**Art and Ashes**
Classic
ISBN 978-3-8174-9493-4

**Cook and Kill**
Classic
ISBN 978-3-8174-9492-7

**Crime Scene Tower of London**
Classic
ISBN 978-3-8174-7687-9

**Deadly Mistake**
Classic
ISBN 978-3-8174-8259-7

**Death Wasn't the Deal**
Classic
ISBN 978-3-8174-9491-0

**Der Rächer von Canterbury**
Classic
ISBN 978-3-8174-7662-6

**Der rote Nebel**
Classic
ISBN 978-3-8174-7574-2

**Ein fast perfekter Coup**
Classic
ISBN 978-3-8174-7568-1

**The Mystery of the Mummy**
Classic
ISBN 978-3-8174-7304-5

# Lernkrimi Lektüren Englisch

**Schüsse im Nebel**
Classic
ISBN 978-3-8174-7763-0

**Tod eines Dandys**
Classic
ISBN 978-3-8174-7660-2

**Toxic Testament**
Classic
ISBN 978-3-8174-7879-2

**Inspector Hudson Investigates**
Sammelband 3 in 1
ISBN 978-3-8174-7625-1

**London Crime Time**
Sammelband 3 in 1
ISBN 978-3-8174-7787-6

**Bone by Bone**
Lernthriller
ISBN 978-3-8174-9497-2

**Massacre United**
Lernthriller
ISBN 978-3-8174-9319-7

**Faceless Killer**
Lernthriller
ISBN 978-3-8174-8856-8

**Bloody Diamonds**
Classic
ISBN 978-3-8174-9494-1

**Das geheimnisvolle Gemälde**
Classic
ISBN 978-3-8174-7306-9

**Der Seelenjäger**
Classic
ISBN 978-3-8174-7581-0

**Der unheimliche Ritter**
Classic
ISBN 978-3-8174-7661-9

**Die Rache des Lords**
Classic
ISBN 978-3-8174-7663-3

**Die Spur des Höllenhundes**
Classic
ISBN 978-3-8174-7307-6

**Lady Mayfair's Revenge**
Classic
ISBN 978-3-8174-7815-6

**Nobody Dies Twice**
Classic
ISBN 978-3-8174-9495-8

**The Riddle of the Black Shoe**
Classic
ISBN 978-3-8174-7638-1

**Schatten der Vergangenheit**
Classic
ISBN 978-3-8174-7570-4

**Teuflische Intrigen**
Classic
ISBN 978-3-8174-7608-4

**In Terror**
Lernthriller
ISBN 978-3-8174-8857-5

**A Scottish Murder Mystery**
Classic
ISBN 978-3-8174-8379-2

## Lernkrimi Hörbücher Englisch

**Dangerous Deals**
ISBN 978-3-8174-9988-5

**A Shot in the Night**
ISBN 978-3-8174-8202-3

**Death Wish**
ISBN 978-3-8174-8204-7

**The Butterworth Mystery**
ISBN 978-3-8174-8203-0

**Strangled**
ISBN 978-3-8174-9665-5

**Bloody Revenge**
ISBN 978-3-8174-8860-5

**Danger at King's Cross**
ISBN 978-3-8174-7673-2

**Bloody Legacy**
ISBN 978-3-8174-7676-3

**Crime & Company**
ISBN 978-3-8174-8976-3

**Die Intrigantin**
ISBN 978-3-8174-7675-6

**Murder at the Office**
ISBN 978-3-8174-7747-0

## Lernkrimi Rätselblöcke Englisch

**Murderous Games**
ISBN 978-3-8174-9500-9

**The Art of Crime**
ISBN 978-3-8174-9155-1

**A Deadly Puzzle**
ISBN 978-3-8174-8832-2

## Lernkrimi Sprachkurs Englisch

**Lernkrimi Sprachkurs**
ISBN 978-3-8174-7844-5

# Compact Lernkrimi
## Spannend Sprachen lernen

### Compact Lernkrimi Lektüren

- Spannende Krimistorys mit zahlreichen Übungen
- Vokabel- und Infokästen direkt auf der Seite
- Durchgehende Geschichte oder drei Kurzkrimis

ab 7,99 € (D)

### Compact Lernkrimi Sammelband

- Drei Lernkrimis in einem Band mit über 300 Übungen
- Für mittleres bis fortgeschrittenes Sprachniveau
- Auch Sammelband Kurzkrimis erhältlich

12,99 € (D)

### Compact Lernkrimi Lernthriller

- Hochspannende Thriller mit Gänsehaut-Garantie
- 70 Übungen mit ansteigendem Schwierigkeitsgrad
- Vokabel- und Infokästen

7,99 € (D)

### Compact Lernkrimi Hörbuch

- Krimistory auf CD mit MP3-fähigen Tracks
- Gelesen von Muttersprachlern
- Begleitbuch zum Mitlesen inklusive Übungen und Vokabelangaben

9,99 € (D)

### Compact Lernkrimi Sprachkurs

- Sprachen lernen für Anfänger
- Krimigeschichte in 10 Lektionen
- Vokabelkarten zum kostenlosen Download

14,99 € (D)

### Compact Lernkrimi Rätselblock

- Mini-Krimis mit vielen Rätselübungen
- Lösungen und Vokabelangaben auf der Rückseite
- Zahlreiche Illustrationen

5,99 € (D)

Englisch | Französisch | Italienisch | Spanisch
Deutsch als Fremdsprache | Schwedisch | Niederländisch

www.lernkrimi.de
www.compactverlag.de
www.facebook.com/lernkrimi